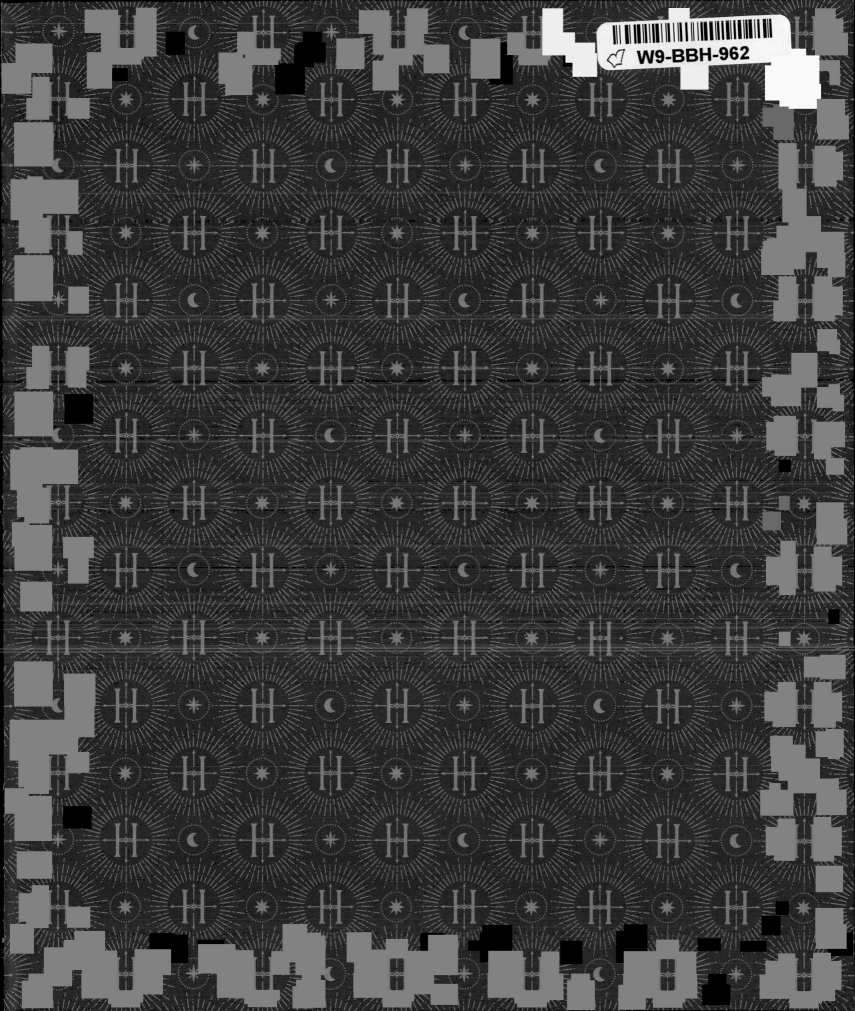

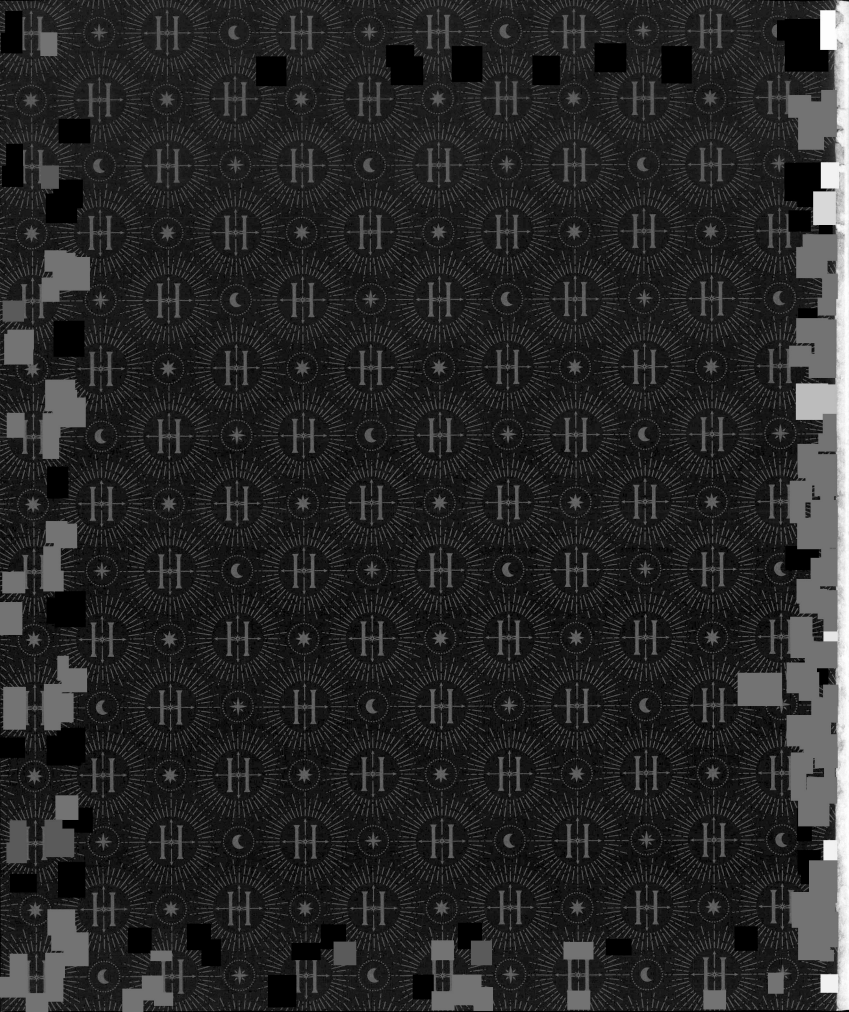

HARRY POTTER
AND THE
CURSED CHILD

THE JOURNEY

Harry Potter
AND THE
CURSED CHILD

· ✳ ·

THE JOURNEY

BEHIND THE SCENES
OF THE
AWARD-WINNING

STAGE PRODUCTION

Based on an original story by
J.K. ROWLING, JOHN TIFFANY & JACK THORNE

·

A Play by
JACK THORNE

·

Produced by
SONIA FRIEDMAN PRODUCTIONS, COLIN CALLENDER &
HARRY POTTER THEATRICAL PRODUCTIONS

· ✳ ·

Foreword by   *Written by*
J.K. ROWLING   JODY REVENSON

SCHOLASTIC INC.

Published by Scholastic Inc., *Publishers since 1920.*
SCHOLASTIC and associated logos are trademarks and/or
registered trademarks of Scholastic Inc.

Library of Congress Cataloging-in-Publication Data
available

ISBN 978-1-338-27403-5
10 9 8 7 6 5 4 3 2 1   19 20 21 22 23

Printed in China   62
First edition, November 2019

Book design by Paul Kepple and Alex Bruce at
Headcase Design
www.headcasedesign.com

This book was edited by Emily Clement. The production
was supervised by Erin O'Connor and Melissa Schirmer,
and the manufacturing was supervised by Joe Romano.
Special thanks in the production of this book to Meg
Massey, Elizabeth Shackelford, Kate Eastham, and
Shannon Kingett of Sonia Friedman Productions; and
Natalie Laverick of The Blair Partnership.

CONTENTS

FOREWORD

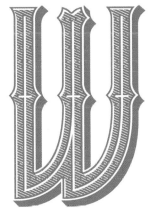

HEN PRODUCERS SONIA FRIEDMAN AND Colin Callender first proposed their idea for a new play, exploring the themes of family and loss at the heart of the Harry Potter stories, I was intrigued. For years I'd turned down proposals to adapt the books for the stage, but this was something different, something new.

If there's one thing I've learnt in life, it's all about the people you work with. So, when Jack Thorne and John Tiffany were brought into the team to develop the story with me, I knew I could trust them to create something truly extraordinary.

I have so many wonderful memories of the earliest rehearsals, of seeing the costumes and illusions for the first time, but what I remember most fondly about the three of us working together is the laughter. I loved the process from beginning to end.

Collaborating on *Harry Potter and the Cursed Child* has been one of the most rewarding experiences of my working life and I could not be prouder of what we achieved. There is a power in live theater that cannot be replicated in any other art form, and sharing the story with an audience for the first time was a breathtaking experience I will never forget. I'm thrilled that the magic can now be shared with audiences around the world.

—*J.K. Rowling, 2019*

✷ B·E·G·I·N·S ✷

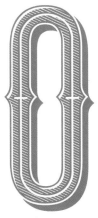

"UR FIRST MEETING WITH J.K. Rowling was not just a meeting about story," producer Sonia Friedman recalls. Producer Colin Callender agrees: "It wasn't really about business arrangements, or would it be one part or two parts—it was a meeting about parents."

It was autumn 2013, and Friedman and Callender had arranged a meeting with Rowling through her agent, Neil Blair, to discuss the possibility of a live theatrical stage production based on Harry Potter. They knew this wasn't the first time Rowling had been approached about bringing Harry Potter to the stage—there had been proposals of Harry Potter musicals, stadium shows, Harry Potter on Ice . . . Rowling had turned them all down. But what idea might spark the author's interest?

Sonia Friedman and her company, Sonia Friedman Productions, have been responsible for some of the most successful theater productions in London and New York. Since 1990, SFP has developed, initiated, and produced over 170 new productions and together the company has won a staggering 55 Olivier Awards, 24 Tonys, and 2 BAFTAs. "I'm in love with all the genres of theater," says Friedman, "but at the very epicenter of it is new writing and storytelling. Everything else spirals around it, but new work, new writing, and new plays are ultimately my oxygen." As an Emmy, Golden Globe, and BAFTA winning producer, Colin Callender was one of the leading forces of the British independent television production sector. As president of HBO Films, Callender played a central role at a time of great commercial and critical success before forming Playground Entertainment in 2012.

Their shared appreciation and support for new work informed the approach the producers took when brain-storming a potential Harry Potter project. "We both knew, without question, it was never going to be an adaptation of the books," says Friedman. "That was not interesting to us. Let's do a new play, a new story inspired by the themes and ideas around the Harry Potter stories."

The producers initially saw this as an intimate character drama, not an adventure driven by narrative and action. "We wanted to think about this as a play that could actually first be seen at the Royal Court Theatre, a real proper play," Callender explains. "At the same time, we kept coming back to this idea that we were never going to be able to compete with the big visuals of the movies," he adds. "Our intent, really, was to explore the psychological, emotional landscape of Harry, grown up.

{ *previous page* }

From left,
Tom Milligan
(James Potter),
Christiana Hutchings
(Lily Potter),
Jamie Parker
(Harry Potter),
Poppy Miller
(Ginny Potter),
and Sam Clemmett
(Albus Potter)
in the Original
West End Production

{ *right* }

Producer
Sonia Friedman

How did this boy—this boy living under the stairs who didn't know who his parents were, who didn't know he was a wizard, with an aunt and uncle and cousin who were awful to him—how did that boy grow up to be an adult and a father?"

"I think we came to it from completely different angles," Friedman says. "Colin came to it as a father, and I came to it as the daughter of an absent father. But 'father' was the center. That was our way in."

· ✳ ·

AS FRIEDMAN AND CALLENDER approached the street in Edinburgh where they would meet with Rowling, Friedman was suddenly bombarded with memories of her father, Leonard Friedman, who had died in 1994 in Edinburgh. In fact, she knew he had passed away only a few streets from where this meeting was to take place.

Friedman admits she had a bit of a meltdown: "Colin pushed me through the door and said, 'Work with this, keep going, this is all meant to have happened in this way, don't try and hide it.' So, in we went. And that was how the meeting started, with me apologizing for being so emotional, because I was just reliving my dad's death."

Parents, children, and how they relate to one another was an apt topic of conversation for a Harry Potter–related meeting, and was key to the themes Friedman and Callender were looking to explore in a Harry Potter stage production. "I don't know how long the meeting

lasted, but it was a good couple of hours," says Callender. "First it was about connecting with Jo and her understanding where we were coming from; how, with this play, we wanted to tell a new story—not an adaptation, not even a prequel. And second, she needed to meet us in person and feel that she would be in trustworthy hands."

"I had always been quite resistant, if I'm honest, to the idea of putting Harry Potter onstage," J.K. Rowling has said, recalling her first meeting with Friedman and Callender. "And I'd always said Harry's story with Voldemort is done, it's over. So it had to be something really remarkable to make me change my mind. And then Sonia and Colin came to me with a proposal that I really liked."

The producers left the meeting feeling hopeful that they had gained Rowling's trust. "I think that with the combination of Sonia's body of work as a theater producer and my body of work as a film and television producer, she'd seen the quality of what we'd both done and the subjects we'd tackled," says Callender. "I don't think at the time we knew for certain whether she was up for doing it, but she was very engaged."

"But it wasn't like, bye, see you at opening night!" Friedman adds. "We first had to figure out the creative team. Jo isn't a playwright herself, of course, so it was very important to find a writer and director she connected with and felt she could work with. If we could accomplish that, it was agreed we'd move forward. It was stage by stage."

"Either through naivety or sheer overwhelming excitement, we didn't feel pressure at that point," says Callender. "But we knew that we had to put together a brilliant creative team, and our starting point was the director."

· ✳ ·

FRIEDMAN'S FIRST THOUGHT, AND Callender agreed, was that they should talk with director John Tiffany. "John's work is very emotionally and physically based; he's not a director you associate with high tech or the modern gizmos out there," Friedman says. "We knew that Harry Potter had to be about storytelling and the magic that's happening before your very eyes."

In addition to being a fan of Tiffany's work for a long time, they had worked together early on in their careers. The first play Tiffany directed, *Gagarin Way*, was also the first play Friedman produced in the West End while at the Ambassador Theatre Group, bringing

{ left }

Producer
Colin Callender

it over in 2001 from Edinburgh's Traverse Theatre, where Tiffany had started his career as literary director. After his time at the Traverse Theatre, Tiffany became associate director of the Paines Plough touring company, which presented new playwrights' work, and then joined the National Theatre of Scotland in 2004 as associate director of new work. Here he directed the Olivier Award–winning production of *Black Watch*, which dramatized the true stories of Scottish soldiers serving in the Iraq War.

"*Black Watch* was one of the most powerful theater experiences I'd ever seen," says Friedman. "You really believed that you were watching these guys at war. And the physicality of it, the emotion and the movement, were so powerful." Callender had also seen *Black Watch*: "It had its own theatrical sleight of hand, and it was that sort of imagination we wanted to capture."

café. "Because of that, Harry Potter's always had a special place for me," says Tiffany. "I'd had a kind of sneak preview. I felt very lucky that I'd seen it before anyone knew what it was, including her."

"At that moment, the hair on the back of Sonia's and my necks literally stood up," says Callender. Later, when Friedman and Callender would introduce Tiffany to Rowling, she commented that he looked familiar. "And then when John told me about the Traverse Theatre connection, that was amazing—it felt predestined," says Rowling.

While Tiffany listened as Friedman and Callender described what they wanted to explore, he experienced some doubts about working on the project. "I thought, I don't know if they've got the right person here, you know?" Tiffany recalls. "I have absolutely no history of doing anything like this. The Broadway musical I did

"WE KNEW THAT HARRY POTTER HAD TO BE ABOUT STORYTELLING AND THE MAGIC THAT'S HAPPENING BEFORE YOUR VERY EYES."

—SONIA FRIEDMAN

Tiffany had also directed the Off-Broadway and Broadway productions of the musical *Once*, winning his first Tony. His final production at the National was *Let the Right One In*, an adaptation by writer Jack Thorne of a Swedish novel and film described as a coming-of-age vampire love story.

Friedman and Callender met Tiffany in London at the Covent Garden Hotel. The chosen room at the hotel had shelves of books, a large fireplace, and cushy red-and-gold furnishings. "We asked him, was he familiar with the books? And he said yes," says Callender. "And then he told this story . . ."

Many years earlier, when Tiffany had just begun working as associate director at the Traverse Theatre in Edinburgh, he often frequented the theater's café. Occasionally, he would see a young woman with a baby, drinking coffee and writing in longhand for hours. In time, they became familiar enough to nod hello to each other. After *Harry Potter and the Philosopher's Stone* was published, Tiffany saw J.K. Rowling being interviewed on television and realized she was the woman from the

was set in a bar with four tables and eight chairs. I thought, somewhere along the line someone's going to want a Quidditch match. Not that that kind of challenge wouldn't excite me, in a way, but I just thought, is this a stadium show?"

The meeting ended with one more piece of synchronicity that might be taken as a sign. As Callender and Friedman left the room shortly after their potential director exited, "We realized it was called the Tiffany room," says Callender. "So between John having met Jo, and now this . . ."

Tiffany continued to meet with the producers to discuss the project and offer his thoughts. It was becoming obvious that the beginning of their new story should be the epilogue from *Harry Potter and the Deathly Hallows*, "Nineteen Years Later." "Our starting point was there, ready and waiting at the end of book seven," says Friedman.

Tiffany agreed that theater could tell this story, "but it had to have a similar epic storyline to the books," he says. "I said we also need to bring evil back, because if it just goes on from the battle of Hogwarts and nineteen years later, then we know there's no jeopardy. Also, we can't go from within the canon, because the audience has to know that it might not be all right, otherwise where are the stakes?" Tiffany was now fully engaged in figuring out how to bring a new Harry Potter story to the stage.

There was one other important determining factor that led to Tiffany accepting the project: The nephews and godchildren he had read the books to over the years told him, simply, that he had to do it.

• ✳ •

ON AN UNUSUALLY WARM JANUARY night in London, John Tiffany and writer Jack Thorne were walking from the Tube to the South Bank Sky Arts Awards, where they were nominated for their achievements in theater with *Let the Right One In*. "We were walking to the awards ceremony," Thorne recalls, "and he said, 'I've been offered Harry Potter.'" News was already out in the theater community (and beyond) that Harry Potter was planning to make a leap onto the stage, "but I didn't ever think that I could be part of it," says Thorne. "So, I went, 'Oh, wow, mate, that's amazing.'" Thorne wasn't sure where the discussion was leading—perhaps Tiffany was asking him about whether the director should do it or not? "And then he went, 'So, I'm going to do it and I would like you to write it if you're up for it.'" Thorne literally slipped off the pavement.

Thorne and Tiffany had first met at Cambridge, where Tiffany was teaching a masterclass. The two kept in touch, "and then the very first thing I had after university with professional actors, John Tiffany directed," Thorne recalls.

Thorne went on to write *When You Cure Me*, his first produced play, which premiered at the Bush Theatre in 2005. The play opened doors to writing in all media for Thorne—stage, radio, television, and film. It was Tiffany who asked Thorne if he would write the adaptation of *Let the Right One In*, which led to their later discussion en route to the awards ceremony.

Sonia Friedman was also up for an award that night. "As it happened, John and Jack won and I didn't," says Friedman, but she met up with Tiffany in the foyer of the awards venue. "John said, 'I'd like you to meet Jack Thorne,'" she remembers. "We didn't talk about Harry Potter at the time, but I met this beautiful, shy, very modest, very tall man who just said, hi, hi, hi, hi."

Shortly afterward, Tiffany told the producers he wanted Thorne to write the play, and a meeting was put together. "Frankly, there was no second thought," says Callender. "It was obvious that Jack and John together were going to be a great match. And there's something madly engaging about Jack as an individual.

"A lot of Jack's work was about younger characters," Callender continues. "And a great thing about his writing is the way he moves between the serious and comedic moments; he intertwines them so that the jokes come at the most unexpected points, or the serious bits emerge out of some of the lighter moments. That's sort of seamless in his plays and part of the strength of what's onstage."

The producers were well aware of Thorne's talents, but there was one more quality that made him a perfect fit. "Jack loves Harry Potter," says Friedman. "He had of course consumed the books, and it turned out that he saw every film many, many times and was, I guess, a superfan."

In his first meeting with the producers, Thorne recalls Friedman saying, "'I listened to the Stephen Fry Harry Potter audiobooks with my stepchildren, John read Potter to his nephews and his godchildren, you read Potter to yourself.' And I *am* that fan—it's me," he says. "I'm a Potterhead, and the idea of getting to play in this universe is still bewildering to this day. Daunting, terrifying, exciting . . . It was sitting in a space rocket and you've got to go—and by the way, we've got a year and a half to get the script right."

"It was very clear that Jack, himself, had a personal connection to the storytelling," says Callender. "And then John and Jack went up to go and meet Jo, and she fell in love with them."

• ✳ •

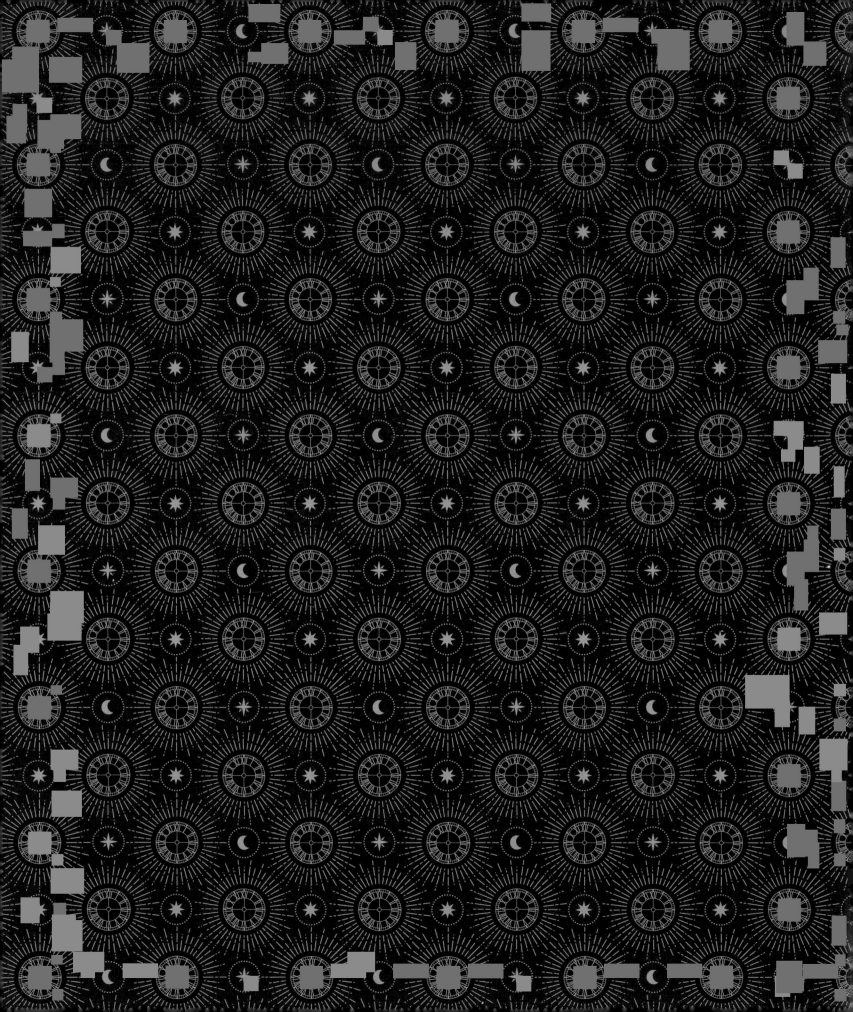

CHAPTER

I

DEVELOPING THE

STORY

brings his body back, it's just heart-wrenching," says Tiffany. "The most unnatural thing in the world is to outlive your kid." Cedric's death would have left a deep impression on Harry in numerous ways. "That was the first death Harry was responsible for," says Thorne. "Well, he wasn't responsible for *anyone's* death, but he took Cedric there. He was responsible in a Harry way."

The playwright also appreciated *Goblet's* structure. "There's three tasks," he explains. "That's very useful. *Goblet* had lots of stuff going for it. So, when we went up to see Jo for the first time, we went armed with that book."

• ✳ •

IN APRIL 2014, TIFFANY AND THORNE flew up to Edinburgh to see Rowling. Tiffany remembers a moment of trepidation as he introduced Thorne to her. "Suddenly, I thought to myself, 'What if they don't get on?' But within four seconds, I was like, 'Hello? *Hello?*'" Rowling has said, "Jack's just one of my people, I knew instantly. He's phenomenal, emotionally understanding, and totally unafraid to go into the dark place."

Rowling brought them to her writing room, where their first meeting lasted the entire day. "Jack, John, and I knew what we wanted to do emotionally," Rowling has said, "and we discussed ideas I already had about what might have happened next." She explains further: "I was fascinated by Albus as I wrote the *Deathly Hallows* epilogue, and felt a real pull to go with him to Hogwarts." Tiffany and Thorne shared with Rowling their idea to make connections with both the plot and the emotional fallout of *Goblet of Fire*. "It's Harry's first death," says Thorne, "and dealing with Cedric and what Cedric meant . . . It was a transformative year for Harry. So, what if we put Albus and Scorpius in that year, in their fourth year at Hogwarts?" Rowling has said, "The three of us developed this story together, always, I feel, with our eye on family, loss, what it means to be a father, and what it means to be the child of a very unusual father."

Thorne had questions for Rowling beyond what was in the books in order to be able to shape the story. "I think most of what I found out, and was excited by, I got into the play. Such as, what is Hermione doing now? You sort of knew that Harry was going to become an Auror," says Thorne. "Where Hermione ended up was really fascinating to me."

• ✳ •

F RIEDMAN, CALLENDER, TIFFANY, and Thorne had all agreed that the jumping-off point for the play should be the epilogue of *Deathly Hallows*. "We felt sure that the first scene of the play would be the final scene of the last book," says John Tiffany. "That came naturally." But after making that leap, where would they land? At their next meeting, they looked again at what was happening in that final scene at the train station and who was present. To Jack Thorne, it was notable that Rowling had put Draco Malfoy's son and Harry Potter's younger son in the same year at Hogwarts: Clearly they were destined to meet and, like their fathers before them, would have an impact on each other's lives. "And as soon as those two were together, it put the dual father-son relationships into relief," says Thorne.

Tiffany and Thorne didn't want a whole new story about getting to know Harry. "We wanted it to be about where Harry was now, and the scars that accompany him from that time," says Thorne. "What happens to a kid when they don't have any parental support, and they're entrusted with the world? How do you come out of that with any sense of sanity?"

They also wanted the plot to tie into something in Harry's early life. "The story that Jack and I both loved was *Harry Potter and the Goblet of Fire*," says Tiffany. "For the first time, the world opens. The characters are maturing and the world is expanding." In wanting the drama to revolve around Harry as a father to Albus, *Goblet of Fire* offered another father-son relationship that would create a contrast. "The scene of Amos Diggory, when he finds out that Cedric's been killed, when Harry

THORNE DRAFTED A FORTY-FIVE PAGE treatment, and conversations among the team continued, especially between Thorne and Rowling. "We kept talking, talking, talking," says Thorne. "It was a mixture of 'Could we try this?' and her going, 'Ooh, that makes me think of this.' It was a constant deep-core 'mining.' The thing is to shake the author for as much information as possible because their knowledge is your secret weapon, and their knowledge isn't always on paper.

"And this is not hyperbole: She is without doubt the most supportive writer I've ever worked with," Thorne states. "Not that she would say yes to everything. It was in the way she would guide and help and be there." Thorne and Rowling would bounce ideas back and forth on email when he wrestled with something. "She consistently made it easy and not seem like it was the hugest job in the world, which of course it was."

Thorne revised his treatment several times before it went to script, constantly rereading and circling back to *Goblet*. "Most times during this process, a writer delivers a draft, you give them notes, and you get the next draft," says Colin Callender. "And it's one step forward and two steps back. Well, Sonia and John and I would give notes to Jack, and every time the next draft would be an advance—it never went back. Every draft, the play got better and better."

As the story development progressed, Thorne and Tiffany realized that—much like the epic adventures of the Harry Potter novels—the adventure they were crafting with Rowling for the play went beyond the scope of the typical stage production. "So we went to Sonia and Colin, and they said, 'Why don't you do it in two parts?'"

Tiffany recalls. "We didn't think through any of the practical implications at the time, which we have since had to embrace for all its complexity," says Callender. "But we didn't even think twice about it."

• ✳ •

THORNE HAD ONE PARTICULAR IDEA that was important to him to weave into the story. "I really wanted to get into what it's like at Hogwarts when you don't fit in," he states. "One of the first conversations Jo and I had was about the fact that we both found school excruciating. I said I thought that ten or eleven might be the hardest age for a kid, because that was the age I realized it was possible I might not have any friends. That was the age when I thought, this is possibly the moment when I'm going to be on my own."

This fear of not fitting in draws directly from the *Deathly Hallows* epilogue, as Albus voices his concerns about being sorted into Slytherin. It also manifests in the most prominent "new" character in *Cursed Child*: Scorpius Malfoy. While Scorpius is introduced in the epilogue, it's only in *Cursed Child* that his character is explored. Albus meets Scorpius onboard the Hogwarts Express, where Harry met Ron and Hermione. It's apparent that Scorpius is sweet and smart and does not seem to fit the Malfoy mold. Rather, he's a geek about Hogwarts history, worries about making friends, and wouldn't hurt a fly. "I think people seem to love Scorpius as soon as they meet him," declares Thorne. But the writer admits that there's a lot of himself in the character. "Yes, I wrote myself into Hogwarts. He's much nicer than me, but he's like the kid who really couldn't fit in even if you gave him a crowbar. He doesn't know how other kids function, and I found other kids bewildering. People find him charming—it's nice that it's turned into a celebration of the nerd. But there's also a lot of pain in Scorpius, and that was important to me."

Albus and Scorpius become the closest of friends—a pair of misfits banding together in a life-changing, live-saving friendship. "For me, it was always about friendship and about my desire for a best friend who loved me," Thorne admits. "When you're best friends as kids, it's a stronger relationship than you'll ever have with anyone, because you live in each other's pockets."

• ✳ •

Dear Jo,

Here is a treatment. It's changed a little bit since our discussions, but I think retains most of the stuff—with some other stuff added in. What it doesn't have is any sense of the magic that John Tiffany will throw over the stage, but it's written to allow as much of that as possible. I've loved every second of writing it, undoubtedly my most daunting job, but one that has brought me so much joy. I hope you like some of it, there's so much that will change.

Jack

Dear Jack—

Wow.

I love it. I really do.

You've so got the measure of the characters and where the story needs to take us. I'm truly blown away by it.

My one second thought is Marazion. I think we should have a very elderly McGonagall instead. What do you think? Other minor points for discussion can be done face-to-face but I think it's wonderful as it is and really couldn't be happier.

Looking forward to seeing you—thank you and congratulations!

Jxx

Dear Jo—

You have no idea what this e-mail means to me. I've felt like such an imposter in your beautiful world and I so just wanted to do you and Harry justice. And the fact that I've pleased you—that's just awesome. Awesome awesome awesome.

I love the idea of an elderly McGonagall. I think that'd be marvellous. And I truly can't wait to talk about it face-to-face.

I have so loved doing this, and I love how long the road looks ahead, and I promise I'll do everything in my power not to let you down.

Thank you thank you thank you,

Jackxx

THROUGH THE PROCESS OF STORY development, characters came and went, always in the interest of better serving the story. "Obviously there were lots and lots of dramaturgical and narrative changes, but I think we always knew the characters we wanted," says Friedman. "I wanted Dobby in it, but that didn't happen. And we talked a little bit about whether Sirius Black could be there or not." To all involved, it couldn't just be a roll call of Harry Potter characters. "That was an ongoing dialogue all the way through," says Callender. "Everyone had a favorite character, and there wasn't room to have everybody in it."

"They had to have a part in the narrative; there has to be a purpose for them being there," says Friedman. "We had the conversation about who we couldn't tell this story without. Of course, there's a number of characters we couldn't fit in. But we certainly never had a major character cut."

Not cut, but it might have taken a little time before one appeared. In Thorne's original treatment, the headmaster of the school was a professor named Marazion. After Rowling read the treatment, she sent an email back to him. "It was just lovely," says Thorne, "but had one big note in it which was: I think Marazion doesn't fit. I think we need Professor McGonagall."

Additional family members make an appearance on platform nine and three-quarters during the epilogue to *Deathly Hallows*: Hermione and Ron's young son, Hugo, and Teddy Lupin, Remus and Tonks's son. Thorne, Tiffany, and Rowling discussed Teddy Lupin's possible involvement at length. "Teddy's an amazing character," says Thorne, "and he really fitted into our world in terms of 'the sins of the parents visiting the children.' But we realized that we just couldn't do service to him. Every character you use, you've got to use them properly. We reached our limit quite quickly without it feeling like cameos." So Teddy Lupin was left out, and it was suggested that perhaps Hugo was being watched by his grandmother Molly, rather than coming to King's Cross that day.

Luna Lovegood made it to the rehearsal phase but not beyond. Thorne originally played with the idea that elements of the story heralding the return of darkness would be accompanied by the smell of cinnamon. "We would have had the smell of cinnamon wafting through the theater," says Tiffany. "Unfortunately, things like that never work because of air-conditioning." Luna would have been sensitive to the smell, and "she would have been in the Ministry of Magic meetings, saying, 'Has anyone smelt the cinnamon?'" says Thorne. "She was being very Luna-y, and very lovely and interesting, but it just felt like an in-joke for the fans who knew Luna. And we were cheapening her by not giving her the space to be brilliant as well as eccentric."

One of the hardest characters to lose, in many ways, was Astoria Malfoy, wife of Draco and mother to Scorpius. Astoria appeared in the first few drafts, but Thorne and Tiffany came to the same realization that there wasn't enough space in the story to do justice to her. "We didn't have time to go into Draco's private world—we could only see Harry's private world," Thorne explains. "We barely see any of Hermione's private world. It was a problem that we had this character and we weren't serving her."

Thorne and Tiffany brought this concern to Rowling. "We pitched to Jo that we wanted Scorpius's mum to be dead, and explained what that did for Draco—being a single parent—and what that did for Scorpius to remove her." Rowling thought it was an interesting idea and even gave them the illness that would take Astoria's life: a blood malediction.

Without Astoria, Draco and Scorpius lost the emotional glue that held them together. "And it just immediately opened up the whole story," says Thorne. "When we talked to Jo at the beginning, learning her thoughts and all the stories she has in her head, Astoria was this very beautiful woman. I miss the fact that we don't get to tell that story, but hopefully there's hints of her in Scorpius."

· ✳ ·

WHILE HE DEVELOPED THE RELATIONship between Harry and Albus, Thorne's attention was caught by what Harry tells his son about his name in the final chapter of *Harry Potter and the Deathly Hallows*: "Albus Severus, you were named after two headmasters of Hogwarts. One of them was a Slytherin and he was probably the bravest man I ever knew." Harry and Ginny's oldest son, James, is named for Harry's father; their daughter, Lily, is named for his mother. "They got family names and he got legacy names," says Thorne. "Okay, being a James or a Lily is tough. But being an Albus, your parents have decided something about you right at the beginning of your life."

The tension that develops between father and son results in a heated confrontation and words are said between them that are immediately regrettable. Thorne chose to write this scene first: "I wanted to make sure I was able to do it." He was well aware that no one other than Rowling had written new Harry Potter stories to that point. "No one else had chosen what he would say. It was a ludicrous responsibility, and I wanted to make sure she was okay with it." When Thorne sent in his first treatment, he included the explosive, hurtful dialogue

between father and son that is a catalyst in the story. Rowling wrote back to Thorne that she loved what he had done. "Which was lovely, amazing, and such a ridiculous relief," says Thorne. "And then in the first draft, I cut that scene out and John said, 'Where's that gone?'"

Thorne had removed the scene because he felt as if he was putting Harry in a very dark place very early on. But Tiffany told him that was the point. "As often is the case in writing, you go to a brutal place, and then you pull yourself back from there, because you get scared," Thorne explains. "John pushed me back to that brutal place, and it was the right decision." He also admits that removing the scene had made writing the rest of the play harder. "And by putting it back, it made everything make better sense."

The fight between Harry and Albus is shocking, but real and relatable. "I know that there's a lot of people who are very uncomfortable that Harry says what he does, but I think it's true," says Thorne, who became a first-time father during the production. "I don't think it makes him a bad man, I think it makes him very confused. He has to be in a dark place from his childhood, and that's the way of exposing it; we had to go there."

The effects of a fight like this between parent and child would be devastating. "You would want to destroy the world," says John Tiffany. "The energy levels of unhappiness and hatred and anger that would be released at that point would be seismic enough to do what happens in *Harry Potter and the Cursed Child*."

· ✳ ·

SONIA FRIEDMAN CALLS THE DEVELOPment process for *Harry Potter and the Cursed Child* "a complete joy and an utter privilege." Friedman clearly remembers when she read the first drafts and saw the names Harry Potter and Dumbledore on the page. "I was reading it in bed—I seemed to always be in bed when I was reading it; it's where I do my best reading—and I could not believe I was reading a script and these names were in this play I might be producing. My geekness was aquivering! I literally was shaking. And when I read the father-son scene from Jack, the key dramatic shift, I just had tears flowing down my cheeks, going, 'Oh my god, we've got a play.' I wouldn't say it's my favorite scene in terms of making me feel good about the world," she continues, "but it's my favorite scene, because it's the scene where I knew we had a play. I remember John saying exactly the same thing the same day: 'We've got a play. We've got a play.'"

· ✳ ·

{ opposite }

Emails between Jack Thorne and J.K. Rowling, on Thorne's original treatment for *Harry Potter and the Cursed Child*

{ next page }

Jamie Parker (Harry Potter) and Sam Clemmett (Albus Potter) in the Original West End Production

HARRY:

You wish me dead?

ALBUS:

No! I just wish you weren't my dad.

HARRY *(seeing red)*:

Well, there are times I wish you weren't my son.

There's a silence. ALBUS nods. Pause. HARRY realizes what he's said.

No, I didn't mean that . . .

—ACT ONE, SCENE SEVEN

{ *right* }

Pages from
director John
Tiffany's notebook,
from the early
stages of story
development

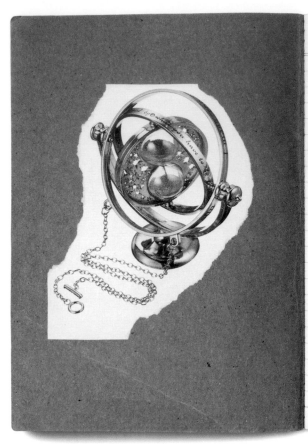

INCREASE IMAGINATION + ADVENTURE

STORY THOUGHTS:

Albus Severus
relationship with HP ... difficult

Has to go back in time — wants to go back
in time?
Horcruxes:
Diary.
Naginni (NL)
Ravenclaw's locket
HP
cup
elder wand, cloak

TRI-WIZARD cup
for dying — if Dobby never gave
Harry Gillyweed ...

Timeturners — Harry has access
because of his job.

POTTERMORE   JULY 8TH 2014

Dumbledore's Army Reunites at Quidditch World Cup Final

By the Daily Prophet's Gossip Correspondent, Rita Skeeter

There are celebrities — and then there are celebrities. We've seen many a famous face from the wizarding world grace the stands here in the Patagonian Desert — Ministers and Presidents, Celestina Warbeck, controversial American wizarding band The Bent-Winged Snitches — all have caused flurries of excitement, with crowd members scrambling for autographs and even casting Bridging Charms to reach the VIP boxes over the heads of the crowd.

But when word swept the campsite and stadium that a certain gang of infamous wizards (no longer the fresh-faced teenagers they were in their heyday, but nevertheless recognisable) had arrived for the final, excitement was beyond anything yet seen. As the crowd stampeded, tents were flattened and small children mown down. Fans from all corners of the globe stormed towards the area where members of Dumbledore's Army were rumoured to have been sighted, desperate above all else for a glimpse of the man they still call the Chosen One.

The Potter family and the rest of Dumbledore's Army have been given accommodation in the VIP section of the campsite, which is protected by heavy charms and patrolled by Security Warlocks. Their presence has ensured large crowds along the cordoned area, all hoping for a glimpse of their heroes. At 3pm today they got their wish when, to the accompaniment of loud screams, Potter took his young sons James and Albus to visit the players' compound,

where he introduced them to Bulgarian Seeker Viktor Krum.

About to turn 34, there are a couple of threads of silver in the famous Auror's black hair, but he continues to wear the distinctive round glasses that some might say are better suited to a style-deficient twelve-year-old. The famous lightning scar has company: Potter is sporting a nasty cut over his right cheekbone. Requests for information as to its provenance merely produced the usual response from the Ministry of Magic: 'We do not comment on the top secret work of the Auror department, as we have told you no less than 514 times, Ms. Skeeter.' So what are they hiding? Is the Chosen One embroiled in fresh mysteries that will one day explode upon us all, plunging us into a new age of terror and mayhem?

Or does his injury have a more humble origin, one that Potter is desperate to hide? Has his wife perhaps cursed him? Are cracks beginning to show in a union that the Potters are determined to promote as happy? Should we read anything into the fact that his wife Ginevra has been perfectly happy to leave her husband and children behind in London whilst reporting on this tournament? The jury is out on whether she really had the talent or experience to be sent to the Quidditch World Cup (jury's back in — no!!!) but let's face it, when your last name is Potter, doors open, international sporting bodies bow and scrape, and Daily Prophet editors hand you plum assignments.

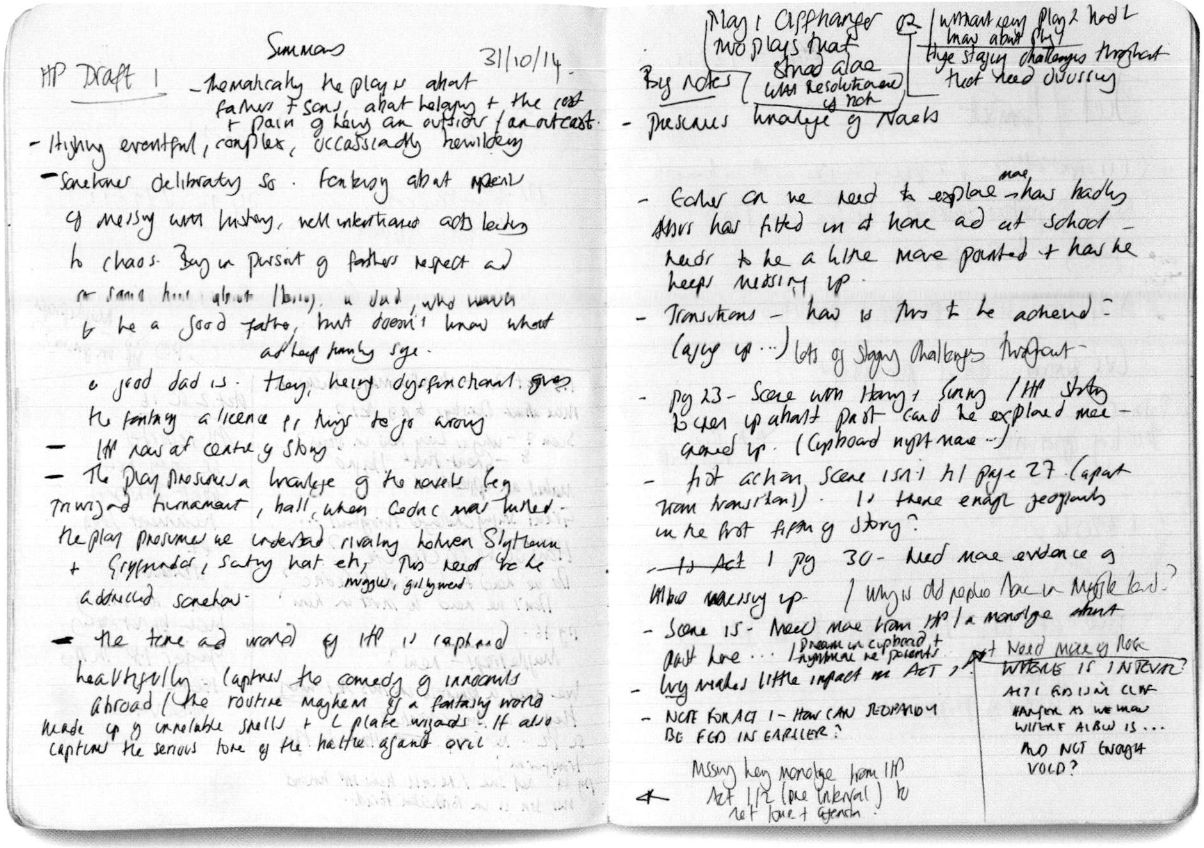
HP Draft 1
31/10/14
– thematically the play is about fathers + sons, about belonging + the cost + pain of being an outsider / an outcast.
– Highly eventful, complex, occasionally bewildering
– The play presumes a knowledge of the novels
– Transitions – how is this to be achieved?
Lots of staging challenges throughout.
– Scene 15 – Need more from HP / a monologue about
– NOTE FOR ACT 1 – HOW CAN DELPHINI BE FED IN EARLIER?
WHERE IS INTERVAL?
Missing key monologue from HP

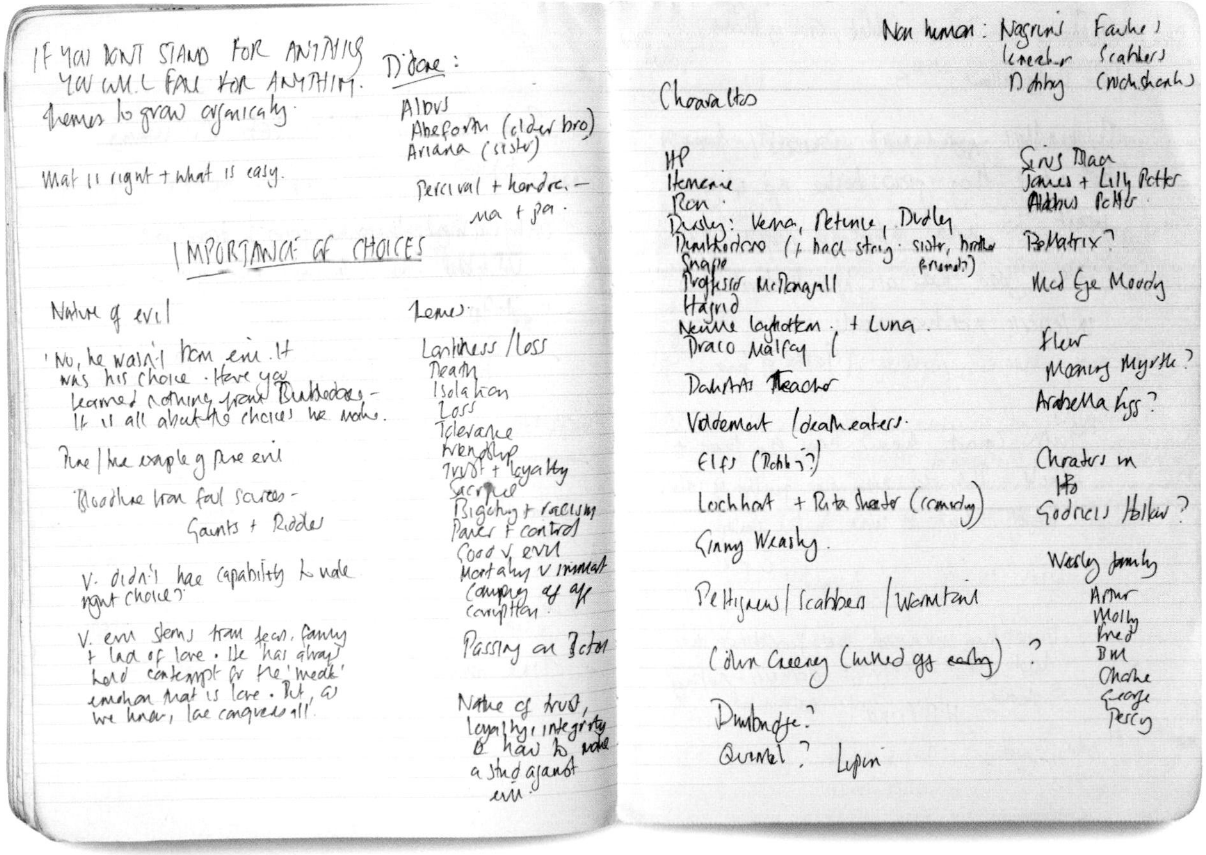
IF YOU DON'T STAND FOR ANYTHING YOU WILL FALL FOR ANYTHING.
Themes to grow organically.
IMPORTANCE OF CHOICES
Nature of evil
Dumbledore:
Albus
Aberforth (older bro)
Ariana (sister)
Themes:
Loneliness / loss
Death
Isolation
Loss
Tolerance
Friendship
Trust + loyalty
Bigotry + racism
Power + control
Good v. evil
Non human: Nagini, Fawkes, Kreacher, Scabbers, Dobby
Characters
HP
Hermione
Ron
Dursley: Vernon, Petunia, Dudley
Snape
Professor McGonagall
Hagrid
Neville Longbottom + Luna
Draco Malfoy
Voldemort / death eaters
Ginny Weasley
Pettigrew / Scabbers / Wormtail
Dumbledore?
Quirrel? Lupin
Sirius Black
James + Lily Potter
Bellatrix?
Mad Eye Moody
Fleur
Moaning Myrtle?
Arabella Figg?
Weasley family
Arthur
Molly
Fred
Bill
Charlie
George
Percy

{ left }

Producer Sonia Friedman's notes on the first draft of Jack Thorne's script

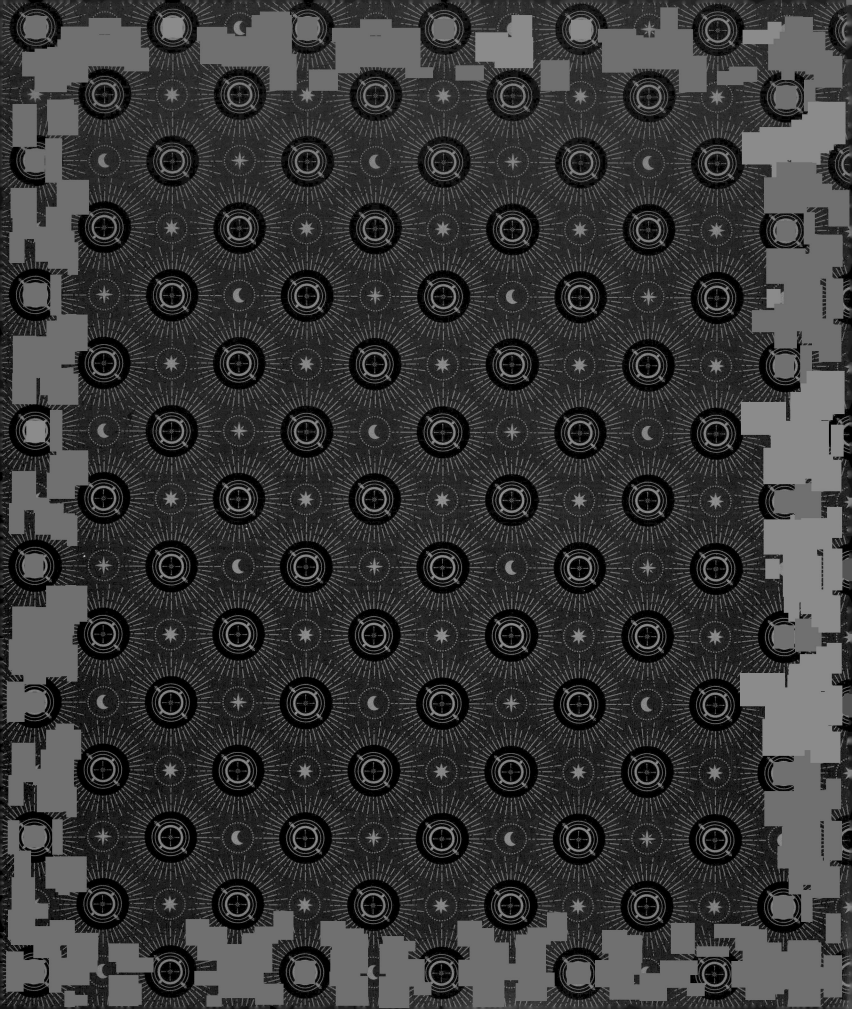

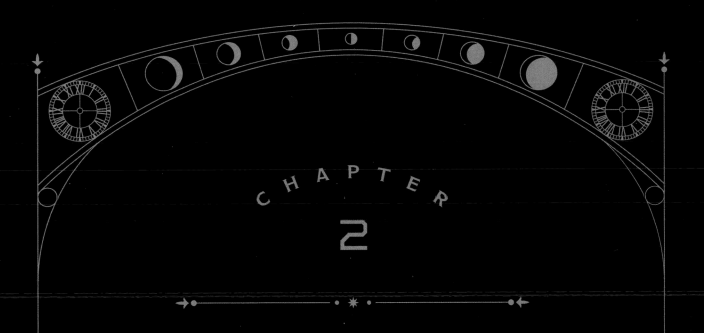

CHAPTER 2

WORKSHOPS AND

REHEARSALS

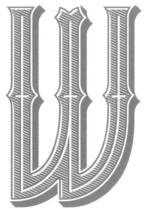

HILE THE SCRIPT CONTINUED TO be finessed, director John Tiffany turned his attention to asking the questions of how the eighth Harry Potter story could be told onstage and putting together the creative team that could answer them. For this, a series of workshops was organized to explore both the story and the possibilities of physically staging the wizarding world. Tiffany describes the workshopping of a play as his laboratory. "There is a symbiotic process happening in terms of a workshop," he explains. "One is the development of the text and the story and the play, and the other is the development of the vocabulary for the staging." For Tiffany, they go hand in hand.

In early February 2015, a small workshop specifically to explore the story for *Harry Potter and the Cursed Child* was held at the Century Club on Shaftesbury Avenue, deep in the West End theater district. The growing team now included set designer Christine Jones and associate director Des Kennedy. Sonia Friedman was very keen to work with Jones, because she had admired *Let the Right One In*. Kennedy had worked with Tiffany on the Dublin and West End productions of *Once*.

The group had a full working script by Jack Thorne at this point, which they could use to identify key elements necessary to serve the narrative and develop initial ideas on how to accomplish these. "We went through Jack's script and talked about it scene by scene," Kennedy remembers. "Everything that could happen or should happen or any queries we had." Friedman and Colin Callender came in and out of the day's meeting, he says, "as they had done lots of work with Jack and John prior to that, but in terms of the creative team getting together and poring through the script and talking about what could potentially be an idea for a moment, this was the first."

{ *right* }

Cherrelle Skeete (center, Rose Granger-Weasley), Chris Jarman (Sorting Hat), and company in the Original West End Production

• ✳ •

{ *above* }

From left, John
Tiffany, J.K. Rowling,
and Jack Thorne
in *Cursed Child*
rehearsals

Illusion designer Harrison recalls, "Everybody was open and giving and generous—making a magic trick work can be quite demanding of the other departments. It can have a huge impact on other designers' work, but Christine and Katrina and Neil and Gareth were all open to the fact that we needed to put a lot of magic in the show, and so it was genuinely a joy."

Austin also took on a unique role for the production: Having never read the Harry Potter books nor seen the films, he was the team Muggle, a valuable resource for ensuring that the production would be accessible to all audience members. "I think it was quite helpul to have someone who doesn't know the canon," says Austin. "You can forget that this show needs to appeal not only to the fans, to the people who love the books, but also to the grandparents who haven't read them and are taking the kids to the show for a treat. Or even the standard theater-goer, who's heard this is a good show, but isn't a Harry Potter fan, and is wondering if it's got anything in it for them."

"My favorite thing about working on the show was what Harry says in the play," says Christine Jones. "He never fights alone, he always has friends. And this was very much like we did it as friends; we had each other to make it happen."

OVER THE COURSE OF THE SPRING AND summer, Tiffany "sorted" the rest of his team. Many of them had worked together previously: Movement director Steven Hoggett had worked with Tiffany and Jones on *Let the Right One In*, and also with Jones on *American Idiot*. Hoggett also had the idea to ask Imogen Heap to compose music for the show, as they had worked together previously. Illusion designer Jamie Harrison collaborated with Tiffany on several productions, including *Peter Pan*. Costume designer Katrina Lindsay and lighting designer Neil Austin worked together on *Bend It Like Beckham: The Musical*, under producer Sonia Friedman. Lindsay also knew Hoggett from various productions. Joining them was sound designer Gareth Fry—a frequent Tiffany collaborator—and production manager Gary Beestone.

The level of collaboration among departments proved to be much greater than is usually needed for a play.

• ✳ •

"MY FAVORITE THING ABOUT WORKING ON
THE SHOW WAS WHAT HARRY SAYS IN THE PLAY . . .
HE NEVER FIGHTS ALONE, HE ALWAYS HAS FRIENDS.
AND THIS WAS VERY MUCH LIKE WE DID IT AS FRIENDS;
WE HAD EACH OTHER TO MAKE IT HAPPEN."

—CHRISTINE JONES

> "WE KNEW WE WANTED
> TO GET BACK TO WHAT IT
> FELT LIKE TO READ
> JO'S BOOKS FOR THE
> FIRST TIME. THEREFORE,
> WE KNEW IT NEEDED TO BE
> RAW, ROUGH THEATER."

—SONIA FRIEDMAN

FROM THE VERY START, THE PRODUCERS knew they didn't want to compete with the computer-generated effects of the eight Harry Potter films. "We knew we wanted to get back to what it felt like to read Jo's books for the first time. Therefore, we knew it needed to be raw, rough theater," says Friedman. "Simple through and through."

"Sonia and Colin had always said 'simple story-telling,' though obviously this isn't simple at all!" says Tiffany. It was also Tiffany's wish that technology not overwhelm the production. Instead, his approach was that "everything that we do, kids have to be able to do at home." With their own imaginations, they could transform via Polyjuice Potion using their parents' big winter coats. They could create the Hogwarts Express out of suitcases. "Because that, for me, is the theater: 'I can do that.'"

Tiffany gave lighting designer Neil Austin the mandate that he did not want to incorporate the classic theatrical "suspension of disbelief." "He said, right from the beginning, this can't be like when you see *Peter Pan* onstage and Peter's on wires and yet we all suspend our disbelief and buy into it," explains Austin.

Sound designer Gareth Fry and associate sound designer Peter Malkin set their own rules to avoid an obvious route for the sounds of spells and charms. "There couldn't be any wind chimes or any sort of clichéd magical sounds," says Fry. "While this show does allow you to leave naturalism behind at times and go into a more imaginative space, the effects still needed to sound real."

Tiffany's philosophies gave a solid approach for the whole team to use. "John was very clear that if you can find the tipping point where you have caught the imagination, the audience will fill in the picture," says Katrina Lindsay. "That's what you need, that's what you want. And I think that's what's so brilliant."

• ✳ •

A DIFFERENT KIND OF WORKSHOP WAS held one week later at Glasshill Studios in London, with Katrina Lindsay, Steven Hoggett, and Brett J. Banakis—associate set designer, working with Jones—joining the group. This workshop featured a few script readings, but it wasn't about the text. "This was about physically working out key moments from the script that would need to become a signature for the production," says Friedman. "Jack and John and Jo had been given license to *go*, because they shouldn't be inhibited by us saying, 'Oh, we can't do that.' Jack put everything down on the page, and then it was John's problem and the creative team's problem to work out how to do it."

The early physical workshops provided that for the production. "Jack had said we were going to be on tops of trains and we're going to have to transform with Polyjuice and confront dementors," Friedman continues. "And how do we do it? How do we do it without technology?"

Over the course of the workshops, she notes, "we created a structure for the team so they asked for materials, they asked for props, they asked for black boxes, they asked for space, they asked whether we could use flame. We organized this time for them, and then we just let them get on with it." At the end of each workshop, they'd share what they'd learned with the producers.

Callender also knew that one of the key jobs he and Friedman had as producers was to create a safe environment so that these questions could be answered. "Protect them from pressures of the outside world and allow talented people to do their very best work," he says. "And that's what we did through the whole process."

• ✳ •

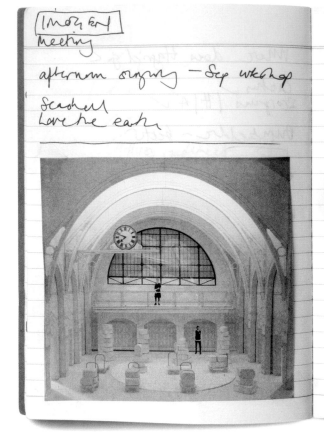

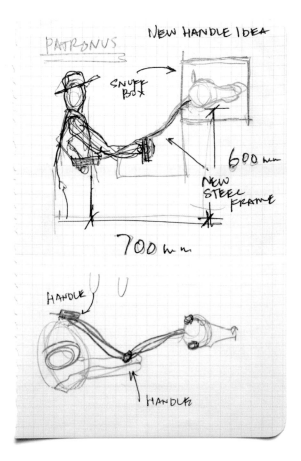

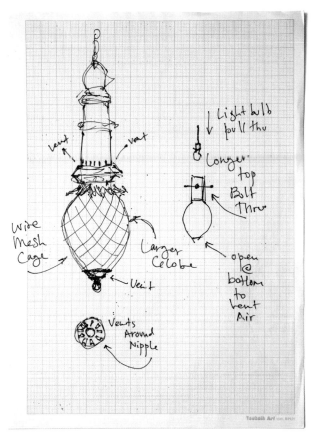

{ above }

Sketches by
scenic supervisor
Brett J. Banakis

{ below }

Sketch of the
chalkboard in
Snape's Potions
class by
set designer
Christine Jones

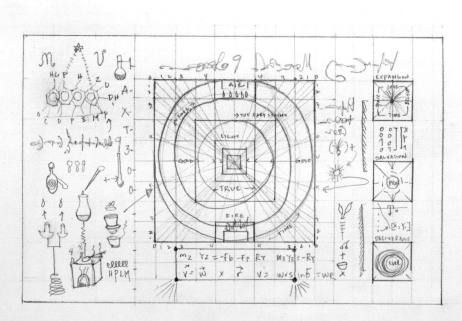

SNAPE POTION'S CLASS

WITH THE THEME OF TRAVEL AND journeying, it was no surprise that suitcases would become one of the most iconic elements of the play. "I remember getting a photograph of King's Cross St. Pancras from John Tiffany," says Friedman. "He said, 'This is my inspiration for the design.' And from that emerged the idea of suitcases—traveling, journeying—and the idea that a suitcase could become a hundred things."

"We looked at life in and out of train stations," says Jones. "What are all the things there? Suitcases and trolley carts and a lot of movement." So, for the first workshop, props supervisors Mary Halliday and Lisa Buckley provided thirty-five suitcases and movement director Steven Hoggett worked with the team on envisioning the physical language of the show.

{ *right* }
Rehearsals for
the Original West
End Production

{ *right center* }
Set designer
Christine Jones
in rehearsal

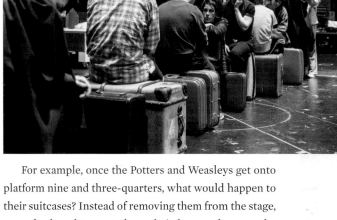

For example, once the Potters and Weasleys get onto platform nine and three-quarters, what would happen to their suitcases? Instead of removing them from the stage, an early thought was to have their luggage become the Hogwarts Express. As Albus Potter and Rose Granger-Weasley board the train, suitcases are arranged all around them, and suddenly the compartments of the Hogwarts Express have been formed right before the audience's eyes, without any fanfare or finger-pointing. Jones describes the "construction" of the train as a "Magic Eye."

Suitcases were the answer not only for the interior of the Hogwarts Express, but its exterior as well. Slipping up to the train's roof, Albus Potter and Scorpius Malfoy encounter the Trolley Witch, who isn't happy they are trying to get off the train. The initial and conventional idea was to build a bridge the train would sit on before the boys leapt off to escape. Jones discussed the idea with Tiffany, but "the bridge was too cumbersome an idea," she says. "We just didn't want to go to that place of giant scenery moving, and set up that vocabulary for

every scene that followed." They realized this was a good opportunity to utilize the suitcases and looked through research photos they had on hand. "We found a picture of just a row of the same color suitcases sitting on the floor, and thought, 'Oh, there's something there.'"

One of Jones's favorite uses of the suitcases is before the play even opens. "When we started thinking about the train station, there was this sense that we actually begin as time is standing still. From the moment the books ended, the world has been standing still." Then a gentleman in a suit comes onstage, "and time starts again. We reenter the world," Jones continues, "and the characters come back to life. In audience terms, for fans, it's literally been just frozen in time, waiting." Suitcases are picked up, and the journey begins.

• ✳ •

JOHN TIFFANY REMEMBERS A BIG PART of the first workshop was "suitcases and cloaks, cloaks and suitcases." Cloaks are a recognizable component of a wizard's wardrobe, and as they had done with suitcases, the team set about figuring out what cloaks could do beyond their function as costumes. Katrina Lindsay brought in university-type gowns, graduation gowns, and travel cloaks rented from different sources to play with. "They just move so beautifully," says Steven Hoggett. "Katrina and I looked at many different varieties and made choices based on the aesthetic."

One inspiration for the use of the cloaks sprang partly from a theme Hoggett was working on that involved birds.

Bird imagery is prevalent in the play, stemming from owls, of course, but is also used in symbolic ways. Very early on, he applied this idea as a way to enable transitions to be made from scene to scene as props and furniture were taken away or added. "Steven planned how the cloaks could become flocks of birds and strike things away," says Des Kennedy. Literally, "striking" the scene.

The cloaks were a perfect costume to create movement, but also to aid in the delivery of the illusions. "Me and Jack and Jo were coming up with story ideas I wouldn't commit to unless I knew that we knew how to solve them," says Tiffany. The workshops proved crucial to solving what ideas would work and how they could accomplish them—one of the most important being the Polyjuice transformation of Albus, Scorpius, and Delphini Diggory, into Ron, Harry, and Hermione.

"Steven, John, and Christine had already talked about this in their earlier meetings," says Lindsay. "How do we do Polyjuice? How do we do transformations? Is there something in this world of wizards and cloaks that allows us to magically disappear things? So, in an early workshop, we practiced different ways people could appear and disappear." By the end of their time at Glasshill, Hoggett, Tiffany, and the other workshop attendees were able to show the producers their first experiments using cloaks to create the Polyjuice illusion. And Tiffany was able to tell Thorne, "Jack, I can do Polyjuice. I went, 'Polyjuice—in. Yeah, we can do that.'"

• ✳ •

SCORPIUS:

So we just take it?

ALBUS:

Scorpius, do I really need to explain to you—
übergeek and Potions expert—
what Polyjuice does?

—ACT ONE, SCENE SIXTEEN

ANOTHER MAJOR SHOW COMPONENT figured out in workshops was finding a way for dementors to take flight. "Katrina and John showed us how a simple torch and a scrap of organza could work," says Friedman. "He literally put the light underneath it and waggled it around. It was all so basic. And I said, 'That's a dementor. That'll do.'"

That scrap of organza was a piece of fabric Lindsay had been carrying around in her bag for years, trying to find the right place to use it. It had been used in a previous production to create a ghostly figure, and she was now considering using it for a dance piece, which is why it was in her bag. "We started talking about the dementors, and I brought out this little scrap," says Lindsay. "It has this incredible movement; it looks like smoke. It's got a lightness and catches the air like no other fabric I know."

Hoggett took a look at the material and had an idea. "Steven suggested we put it on someone and then put a fan on it," says Des Kennedy. "He used his associate Neil Bettles, telling him how to move, and then we turned all the lights out and shone a torch on it and suddenly we had created a dementor."

After this first dementor demonstration, the workshop moved on. "I think you learn through years of working like this that you don't need to see something to its full completion," says Tiffany. "It wastes time. You just need to know that the potential's there and can be worked with." Tiffany also knew that there was only so much time to research and pursue ideas. "I could have spent ages coming up with the dementors sequence, but once we'd got that, there was time better spent in that workshop."

The first attempts at dementors and Polyjuice are pretty much what is seen onstage today. "By usual standards in theater, this process of developing something new normally takes a long time," says Callender. "This happened ridiculously quickly. The point of this workshop was to try and explore, less to do with the script, but more to do with some of the illusions. And things we tried out there are onstage now. It's extraordinary."

• ✳ •

THE NEXT WORKSHOP TOOK PLACE over two weeks in April 2015 at Spectrecom Studios, in Kennington, London. "There had been lots of little bits that were happening aside from the main workshops," says Fiona Stewart, associate producer for Sonia Friedman Productions. "This workshop extended what they'd done in the previous workshop, looking even more at the movement side of things, and then having a script reading." Two early days were devoted to the script prior to the reading, bringing in actors to read aloud sections that Thorne was working on so he could hear it and take that with him as he continued writing.

The illusions and movements developed at the Glasshill workshop were built upon at Kennington. While Lindsay and Hoggett were perfecting ways the cloaks could move with a *whoosh* or a *snap*, sound designer Gareth Fry was finding the actual sounds to use. "When you hear the sound of a cloak," he explains, "you're not hearing the sound of the actual cloak, you're hearing a sound effect." Fortunately, and extraordinarily, Fry already had cloak sounds on file. "I've got a very large library of sound effects," he says with a smile.

But Fry did not have any dementor sounds in his audio files and admits that finding them was a challenge. "Without sound, they're just some floating bits of fabric," states Fry. "There's no dread to that. I spent a lot of time trying to find the sound that had the

"THE POINT OF THIS WORKSHOP WAS TO TRY AND EXPLORE, LESS TO DO WITH THE SCRIPT, BUT MORE TO DO WITH SOME OF THE ILLUSIONS. AND THINGS WE TRIED OUT THERE ARE ONSTAGE NOW. IT'S EXTRAORDINARY."

—COLIN CALLENDER

appropriate amount of horribleness to it and ended up using a mix of horrible shrieks combined with really rattly breathing sounds."

A similar approach was taken to the Polyjuice transformation. "Every aspect of magic that you see in the show has a sonic component," Fry explains. "With Polyjuice, for example, all you see is what they're doing with their voice and body. The thing that takes it from just

somebody gesticulating in a cloak is the sound that's happening with it." The sonic component to an illusion is often intricately involved with the timing of it. As an illusion is being set up or completed, there might be a few moments when visually nothing is happening, and sound is one way to fill that gap.

Illusion designer Jamie Harrison joined the team at this workshop, and Hoggett worked with him to develop the ideas he had had for the Polyjuice transformation. "At the point where I entered, it was very physical theater, and I think what John wanted was for it to be magical," says Harrison. "There were some big scary things we did with that illusion that we didn't know if they would work or not until we got onstage." When it came to that point, Hoggett and Harrison worked with production manager Gary Beestone to codify the illusion. "Gary was always really supportive," Harrison adds, "but also rigorous in terms of questioning everything to make sure that it wasn't a pie-in-the-sky idea."

• ✳ •

ting at the end of a bed or standing in a pool of light," says Callender. "Those are some of the most powerful, moving moments in the play."

• ✳ •

THROUGHOUT THE SUMMER, Thorne continued writing and revising, and having the new pages workshopped in a series of small script-intensive meetings. "There was a mini workshop," says Kennedy, "which was just actors and John and Jack, where it was pulling apart the script. Another just explored the language of the play."

Thorne describes the many read-throughs of the script as "excruciating. But it was so necessary. All the time you're sandpapering off, but particularly in workshops." The writer benefitted not only from hearing his words, but from ideas or concerns of the actors participating in these workshops. "Paul Thornley was in all of them," says Thorne. "So, where Ron is me and Ron is Paul, I'm not sure. It was a real collaboration." Thorne also admits that he drew from members of the creative team as well. "I leached off all of them trying to get the best stuff I could. I leached off Christine Jones, I leached off Steven Hoggett, and we all learned together how to do this play."

After each workshop or mini meeting, Thorne would take the notes and feedback and work on his next draft. "Obviously, the drafts were precious," says Imogen Clare-Wood, production assistant and one of Thorne's supportive "clique of Potterheads," a group that eventually included actor Chris Jarman—the original Sorting Hat and Hagrid—and deputy stage manager Jenefer Tait. Says Thorne, "It was a way of discussing it before I put it in front of John and before I put it in front of Jo. Just checking that I had the right philosophical intent, you know."

"So, once Jack finished a draft, I would go to his house in a car or cab with a memory stick," Clare-Wood continues. "I'd go in, and he would physically put it on the memory stick for me. Then I would come straight back to the office and save it on our system for security." When a copy of the script needed to go to director John Tiffany, Clare-Wood would bring it to him on a memory stick in the same way. Nothing was ever emailed. "And I would sit in the taxi or car thinking, 'I'm carrying around the eighth Harry Potter story.' It was terrifying."

• ✳ •

THE FINAL DAY OF THE KENNINGTON workshop hosted the first, full sit-down read-through of the script. The actors who had been involved in the workshop, which included Paul Thornley and Noma Dumezweni, the original Ron Weasley and Hermione Granger, sat in a horseshoe-shaped ring of chairs around a table, surrounded by the creative team and other production personnel. Friedman's team from SFP was there, as were Rowling and her team. "We had also invited some real Harry devotees, 'superfans,'" remembers Callender, "who weren't part of the theater company or weren't part of the production, and who didn't know what was going to happen, didn't know what the play was or what the story was." Part One was read before lunch; Part Two after lunch.

"And, by the end of that afternoon, after the final scene with Harry and Albus and the play ended, the whole room was in tears," says Friedman. "I remember our production assistant, Imogen, saying, 'It's just like Harry's home again.' And Colin and I looked at each other and said, 'Okay, onward. We're going to do this.'"

After the workshop ended, the emotionally drained company, including Rowling, gathered at a pub around the corner. "And I remember Sonia and Colin saying at that point, 'We're going to find a theater,'" says Tiffany.

It was clear to the producers that the play really worked as a proper play, just with the people sitting around the table, without any of the bells and whistles of the magic and the illusions. "And to this day, some of the most striking moments are really just two characters sit-

CLOSING UP SHOP

• ✳ •

THE FINAL WORKSHOP FOR *HARRY POTTER and the Cursed Child* was held from the middle of September to the middle of October 2015 at Lanterns Studio Theatre, located near Canary Wharf in London. It's also located right above the Lantern Arts Nursery School. "J.K. Rowling came to one of the readings at Lanterns," says Callender, "and I remember Sonia and I thinking, 'If these kids in the school next to us knew who was in this room, they would go nuts!'"

This was the last full workshop before rehearsals would start, so there was still a lot of development happening and scenes were still changing. "The story had basically bedded down by that point, but how we were going to tell the story and do different moments was still up for grabs," says Harrison, who brought in new team member Chris Fisher as illusions and magic associate for the four-week session. "The whole team was still concocting things with each other's skills. There'd be a moment where I'd say, 'We can do that moment with this illusion idea,' or Gareth would say, 'We can say that with the sound,' or Neil would have an idea to do with the lighting."

Meanwhile, there were countless logistical challenges to face in order to take the production from the workshop to the stage. Diane Benjamin (Executive Director, SFP) and Pam Skinner (Executive Producer, SFP) worked around the clock with their team to coordinate rehearsal space and scheduling, negotiate and draft

contracts, and manage the business side of the production, while the marketing team worked to create the show's iconic artwork and build a ticketing system that could handle unprecedented interest for a two-part play. "It takes an army to put on this show, and it was our task to put that army together and ensure that everything was running smoothly," says Skinner. "And of course all these arrangements had to be made in secret," Benjamin adds.

• ✳ •

"IT'S JUST LIKE HARRY'S HOME AGAIN."

——— ✦ ———

—IMOGEN CLARE-WOOD

TIFFANY'S GOAL WAS TO BE ABLE TO GO through the bulk of the show by the end of the Lanterns workshop. "What I *said* was, I want to know how you're going to do everything, team, otherwise I'm not going to agree to rehearsals starting," says Tiffany. "I'm not going to start rehearsals not knowing how, for example, we're going to do the fight on top of the Hogwarts Express. Cut to: starting rehearsals not knowing how I was going to do the fight on top of the Hogwarts Express," he says with a laugh. "But, you know, you have to make these edicts as a director."

For a production that was actually two full-length plays, the workshop process was surprisingly quick. Throughout it, the script and characters grew in development by Thorne, Tiffany, and Rowling. At the same time, Tiffany's "laboratory" yielded nearly finalized illusions and magic, and choreographed movements by Hoggett for cloaks, suitcases, dementors, and Polyjuice transformations. "It's amazing I'm still sane," he says with a laugh. But much had to be devised in the workshops in order to get to the rehearsal phase, and everyone was happy to work as hard as needed.

• ✳ •

{ *right* }

Noma Dumezweni
(Hermione Granger),
in rehearsal

CASTING HEROES

• ✳ •

WORKSHOPS ARE NOT NECESSARILY cast with actors who are the most appropriate for the roles, but ones the production feels at the time will be able to contribute to the project. "We tried to cast actors with the best minds, because it was a new script," says Kennedy. "We might bring in a great English actor to workshop Hagrid, but he's five foot five. So, his brain was good for the purposes of the workshop, but sadly he would never be cast in the part."

However, many of the actors who participated in the workshops had worked previously with Tiffany or Friedman in some capacity, and were ultimately cast in the leading roles. Before February's Glasshill gathering,

knew I loved Noma as a performer, and she just seemed to have that majesty, Hermione's intelligence and strength."

Tiffany explains that there has been a conversation going on in theaters in London and other cities for a while now about diversity in casting. "You do have to have an ambition to be diverse," says Tiffany. "But I think we have to make bold gestures like this. I don't care what people call it; I don't care whether they think it's positive discrimination, or über-liberalism, this is what's happening. The world has changed." Tiffany also felt that casting a black actress as Hermione would mark the play as being clearly different from the films. "It would carve out our own space."

Unavailable for the Glasshill workshop, Dumezweni started at Kennington. "That outsider girl, I know that girl who works hard to try and achieve," says Dumezweni. "There are so many kids of color who go, 'I'm Hermione,' because you're an overachiever, or you're from an immigrant family, or any other thing."

> ## "I KNEW THAT I DIDN'T WANT ALL THREE CHARACTERS TO BE WHITE IN THE STAGE VERSION... [NOMA DUMEZWENI] JUST SEEMED TO HAVE THAT MAJESTY, HERMIONE'S INTELLIGENCE AND STRENGTH."

—JOHN TIFFANY

actor Paul Thornley received a call from his agent, who asked if he could participate in a workshop for Friedman, with whom he'd worked before. "He said, 'We can't tell you what it is, just go and read it,'" he remembers. When Thornley took a look at the script and saw that it had something to do with Harry Potter, he asked what part he'd be reading. "When they said Ron, I said, 'Okay—but I'm really old.'" Fortunately, once he'd read the script, it made more sense. Thornley ended up workshopping Ron from Glasshill to Lanterns.

Actress Noma Dumezweni, who read Hermione Granger, had been in previous workshops for Tiffany, but their schedules had never meshed for him to cast her. "I'd known her since the nineties," says Tiffany. "She did a one-woman show at the Traverse Theatre, which is where I'd first encountered Jo. All full circle. And she was wonderful." Tiffany had Dumezweni in mind for the part from the very beginning. "I knew that I didn't want all three characters to be white in the stage version," he explains. "I

Actor Alex Price had never done any workshop prior to being asked by Tiffany to read Draco Malfoy at Lanterns. Price was already excited about working with Tiffany, Hoggett, and the rest of the team; then he read the script. "There've been lots of times when I read a script, and I've had no idea what's going on and how it's going to work," he says. "But Draco's journey and story were as clear as day, and I also felt I could offer something. And I wanted to."

Price was there for the full four weeks, not just workshopping Draco; he also worked with Hoggett and Tiffany on movement for scenes that didn't involve that character. "It's a weird situation," he admits. "You fall in love with the people that you're working with, the material that you're working on, but you haven't been offered the job. That's hard."

• ✳ •

{ *above* }

J.K. Rowling
with director
John Tiffany,
the producers,
and the
production team
on the first day
of rehearsals

{ *right and opposite* }

The Original West
End Company in
rehearsal

AS THE WORKSHOPS CAME TO AN END, it was time to make casting decisions for the forty-three actors needed to fulfill the roles of the play, from Harry Potter himself to the Ministry witches and wizards and Hogwarts students. It had become clear to Tiffany, Friedman, Callender, Thorne, and Rowling, all of whom had a hand in casting, that some of the actors who had workshopped characters were just "no-brainers."

"I think the truth is that Noma Dumezweni was so brilliant in reading Hermione that we didn't even need to look any further," says Callender. "And the same was true of Paul Thornley as Ron."

Poppy Miller was cast as Ginny Potter and Alex Price as Draco Malfoy. Sam Clemmett, who workshopped the role of Albus Potter during the first week at Lanterns, was chosen to play Harry's middle child.

Actor Jamie Parker was cast in the role of Harry Potter. "My agent came to me and asked, 'How do you feel in principle about a year in *Harry Potter* in the West End?'" he remembers. "And I was really confused about so many parts of that . . ." He had a good feeling about the auditions, which doesn't happen to him that often. "I thought, 'If I don't get this, it's because of something completely out of my control, so no hard feelings.' And then it suddenly became real. I thought, 'Harry Potter? This is absolutely mental.'"

An actor to play Scorpius Malfoy proved difficult to find, however. "Scorpius is such an interesting and complex character," says Callender. "And there's so much of Jack Thorne in him—so we really had to get it right."

Casting director Julia Horan found Anthony Boyle, who at the time was still a student at the Royal Welsh College of Music & Drama. "I was more sure of this than anything in my life," remembers Boyle. "It was the most incredible role—I couldn't have not done it."

JAMIE HARRISON AND CHRIS FISHER start off their work for each production company of *Harry Potter and the Cursed Child* with a class: Introduction to Magic. Cast members and technical crew attend, but everyone is encouraged to join.

"They just love seeing 'Introduction to Magic' on the call sheet," says Fisher. "Everyone comes in very excited." In the ninety-minute class, Harrison and Fisher talk about the key elements of magic. "Why it works and how it works," says Harrison, "and what's going to be important in the show. And that the most important thing about good magic is storytelling."

Harrison believes that the class is a good way to let cast and crew feel that they are in safe hands in terms of how the magic is being approached, and that they're not just going to be drilled in the technical side of it. "It's fun, and it's good bonding time," he adds. "It's about the actors interpreting the magic as well as working out what their character's story is for telling this moment. I think that's something actors really appreciate hearing. They don't necessarily want to be told just how to do a trick; they want to be able to embody it in the character they're creating."

Each class begins with teaching the students two or three tricks they can take home and perform for their families or others. "And what's nice is that they'll come in the next day," says Fisher, "and tell us, 'I showed the ball trick to my daughter and she just thinks I'm amazing now.' This introduces them into the world of magic a

{ next page }

Harry Potter and the Cursed Child West End production year-one "class photo," including full cast and creative team (2016)

GOING INTO REHEARSALS AT THE BEGIN-

ning of February at the 3 Mills Studios, in Bromley-by-Bow, was all "cloak and dagger," says Friedman. The facility has a shared space of nine filming stages and nine rehearsal stages and rooms, so the odds of bumping into someone familiar from the theater or film community were great. SFP camouflaged the production by pretending they were rehearsing one of Shakespeare's least popular plays, *Pericles*, "so if you were asked about it, they'd go, 'Oh, how boring,'" says Imogen Clare-Wood, and the subject would usually close quickly. "But they must have thought it was the biggest production of it ever," adds Friedman, "because the rehearsals were just going on and on."

The rehearsal room became the production's own Room of Requirement. Whatever was needed, Friedman and Callender tried to provide. Harry Potter books and DVDs were available around the room, and everyone was encouraged to revisit the source. The props department brought in representations of what the actual set and any furniture and props might be. There were even two milliners on-site working on different shapes for wizard hats.

Atypical for the rehearsal stage, every department was there for the entire ten weeks. Christine Jones felt a sense that they were at their own school for magic. "We were like students, all of us," says Jones, "with string and cardboard, tape and fabric and glitter, and we were there to play and figure things out and learn how to make magic."

• ✳ •

little bit," he continues. "But we remind them, quite honestly, that magic's going to be hard at times, and so you'll need to work on it."

An important part of the first lesson is initiating the idea of keeping the secrets. "When you know how magic is done, it's inherently disappointing," says Harrison. "It's the layering of misdirection and psychology, along with costume and lighting and sound and script—that's where the magic really is. So, we have to make sure that the cast feels as protective over these concepts as we do."

• ✳ •

ANOTHER RESEMBLANCE TO HOGWARTS was that a weekly competition for House Cup was instituted, with the winners receiving a trophy or a treat. Production stage manager Sam Hunter came up with the idea, and at the start of rehearsals, cast and crew were sorted into their Houses (the actors were sorted not according to their character but themselves). "We even had a scoreboard," says Kennedy, who instigated one of the first coups for points. "Day three or so, I said to Neil Bettles and the other Gryffindors that we should all dress in red for Steven Hoggett's warm-up the next morning. Really annoyed the other Houses!"

The competition was on. "If you were late, points were taken off," Kennedy adds, "and everybody became a snitch, and not like Harry Potter's Snitch." Five points were taken for mispronouncing *Voldemort* by ending it with a hard *t. Harry Potter*

and the Cursed Child uses J.K. Rowling's original intention for the pronunciation, which ends with the soft, French-sounding *Vol-de-mor.* Trivia questions would come to mind while rehearsing. "We'd be talking about Hermione as the Minister for Magic, and I'd ask how many female Ministers for Magic there had been," says Kennedy. "Fifty points for getting it right!"

Sam Clemmett—Hufflepuff—maintains that as John Tiffany—Gryffindor—gave out a lot of the points, Gryffindor won a higher percentage. "They were very aggressive in making sure they tried to win every single week," he says. Paul Thornley—Ravenclaw—affirms that the contest was heavily skewed. "There were a lot of high-ranking Gryffindors that always seemed to win every week. I'm not going to name names . . . but Ravenclaws did very badly, that's all I know."

The House Cup tradition continues for each new cast across the globe. The original scoreboard of colored

plastic balls dropped into plastic tubes has been upgraded to an electronic board that lists everyone's House. "It clicks over," says Fisher, "so when anyone gets points, it goes straight up on the board. That way you can see who's winning that week and whether you need to get more points." A presentation for the winning House is held each Saturday, immortalized in a photo of the team holding a cup designed by the props department.

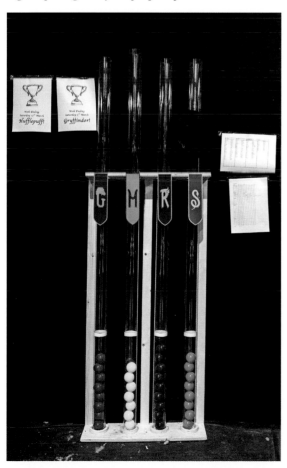

PARTICIPANTS AT THE REHEARSALS were reminded by a sign upon entrance that read *Keep Calm and Keep the Secrets*. "It was exciting that everything was done in secrecy, and that everyone signed up for it," says Friedman. Like the hidden wizarding world in London's Diagon Alley, the show needed to protect itself from Muggles seeing or hearing about it. Fortunately, the people involved in the show found it easier to keep a secret when there were others to share it with without consequences.

"We were in the big warehouse of 3 Mills," says Kennedy. "There was no natural light, and because we couldn't allow the cleaners inside in case they tried to take photos, it was filthy. So, we were like tomatoes in the dark for three months." Kennedy avers it was as easy as it was important to form a community, especially as they were involved in something related to Harry Potter. "But better, we formed a family."

Callender agrees that having to keep a secret created a great communal spirit. "Everyone felt they were in it together," he says, "and that was fun." He admits that it might have been harder for the parents with young kids in the company. His children knew he was working on Harry Potter, "but they didn't know anything about the show. They didn't know what the story was, and we didn't go into details." And even after they'd seen it, Callender would not reveal how the illusions were done.

Thornley struggled with keeping the secret from his daughters but prides himself that at a specific encounter just as the show was starting previews he held fast. While out dining with a friend, he met Dame Maggie Smith. "I was introduced as, 'This is Paul, he's playing Ron Weasley,'" he explains. "She went, 'Yes, I can see that.' Then she asked, 'Am I in it?' And I replied, 'I can't tell you.' I don't think she's ever seen it, but I was able to keep the secrets even from Professor McGonagall!" he says with glee.

Friedman reveled in being a secret keeper. "It was great and one of the best times of my life," she says. "I doubt very much I'll ever be involved with something that will have that level of mystery and excitement and secrecy around it that creates and engenders so much goodwill and excitement from everybody else. These were very, very, very precious times."

• ＊ •

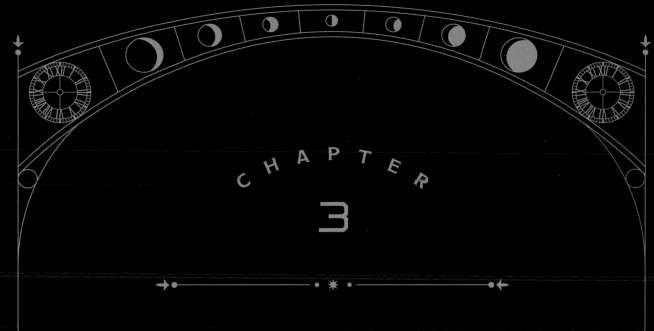

CHAPTER

3

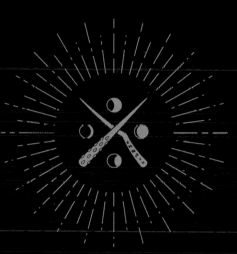

MOVEMENT, MUSIC, AND

MAGIC

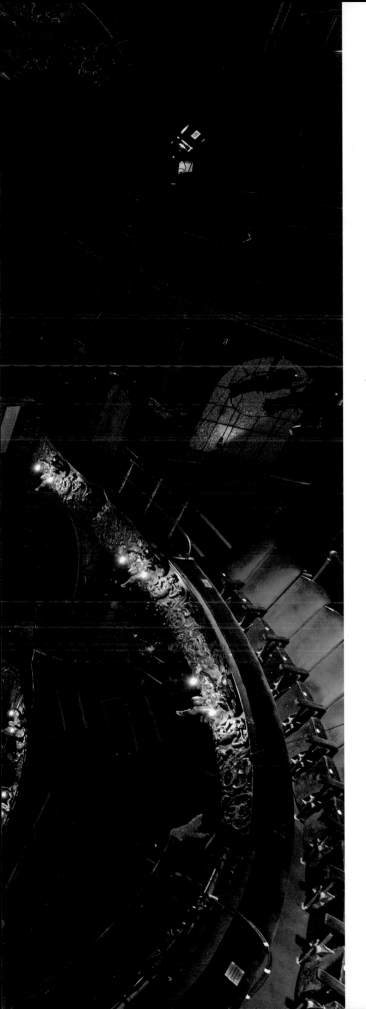

MOVEMENT

THROUGH THE WORKSHOP sessions, director John Tiffany and movement director Steven Hoggett set up a physical vocabulary to stage the production: suitcases that represented travel, cloaks to give flow and cover for the transitions between scenes, doors and stairs and walls to define architecture. Each role has its own physical vocabulary as well. Movement, whether in a scene with two people or a choreographed dance of twelve, must push the story forward, says Hoggett. "Is there choreography in the show? Absolutely there is. But half my job is being in the room so people are just thinking about their physicality."

Hoggett is one of three cofounders of the Frantic Assembly theater company, which creates new productions and revisits great plays incorporating movement and music into the storytelling. He is also longtime friends with John Tiffany. In 2003, while associate director of the Traverse Theatre, Tiffany asked Hoggett to help him with a new play written by Gregory Burke. Collaborations between the friends continued, including Burke's next play, *Black Watch*, for which Hoggett won, among other awards, the Olivier Award for Best Theatre Choreographer. Tiffany and Hoggett also worked on *Let the Right One In* and the Broadway musical *Once*, for which Tiffany and Hoggett shared a 2012 Obie Award special citation with musical director Martin Lowe.

When Tiffany called his friend about *Harry Potter and the Cursed Child* and suggested they work together for what would be the tenth time, Hoggett was deep into creating the fight sequences for Broadway's *Rocky: The Musical*. "The thought of working on something else

{ *left* }

Technical rehearsals at the Palace Theatre, including the Steven Hoggett warm-up onstage

really big was a worry for about a second," he says. "I thought, 'That sounds terrifying.' So, I said yes."

Hoggett assembled his team for the show, consisting of associate movement director Neil Bettles, and Nuno Silva, who began as movement captain, as well as playing Bane in the original London production. Just prior to *Cursed Child*, Bettles and Silva had worked together with Hoggett on *The Light Princess* at the National Theatre. Both have also worked with Frantic Assembly on various productions; Bettles is now associate director of the Frantic Assembly company. Silva is now the UK resident movement director.

WARM-UPS

· ✳ ·

THE PHYSICALITY OF *HARRY POTTER* *and the Cursed Child* is demanding, so starting in workshops, every day the cast, and any crew who want to join in, participated in a "Steven Hoggett warm-up."

"My job is to look at the physical demands of the show and make sure the warm-up prepares your performing company so that they can deal with playing that show for as long as it's running," says Hoggett. He began doing warm-ups with his Frantic Assembly company, because during their first few years, bruises and muscle tears and body aches were more prevalent than he felt they should be. What Hoggett realized was, although they were doing warm-ups, they weren't doing the *right* ones, so he needed to devise what the

best way was to warm up the body. "So, I come to warm-ups as a choreographer now after ten years of having four years of bruises and then six years of not a single bruise on my body."

Hoggett's most important instruction for an actor is to be mindful of his or her body. He reminds them

that there will be times when they won't be able to do what he asks. "And that's okay," he says. "Try it within your capacity. You might *never* be able to do it, but that's also fine. Just be smart about it." Hoggett will call out if someone is pushing too far, or if they're not pushing far enough, "but by asking them to check what their bodies are doing, you're achieving half your goal, to think physically."

While in rehearsals, the physical workouts are different each day and typically run in a pattern over a week. "Wednesdays are yoga-based," says Silva, who taught warm-ups for two years. "Thursdays are circuit Thursdays. A lot of cardio, press-ups and push-ups and sit-ups for circuit training." Friday is "Fun Friday." "We do a bit of choreographed dancing, silly dances, to go through the body to warm up everything. On a Saturday, I would normally teach Tabata, a circuit-like form of high-intensity interval training. On Sunday, I would go back to yoga. I would start the week with yoga, and I would finish the week with yoga, to center everyone again."

Hoggett describes the show as ballistic, "in the sense that the body is doing nothing, then it's doing something, and quite quick: grabbing, moving, throwing, swift movement that also needs to be delicate. And then the body stops for a few minutes," he explains. "Your body needs to be ready to be active at any given time. So, stamina is really important, flexibility's really important." Hoggett would also adjust the work to address specifics that might be on the day's schedule. On days with much "suitcase involvement," Hoggett would do spot work on rotator cuffs. Other days, when the focus was on a choreographed piece, the warm-up would include something very count-laden.

Actor Paul Thornley credits Hoggett with making him a much fitter man. "The first warm-up I remember doing a full-on fitness class for an hour. And the next morning I could barely get up the escalators at the Tube. That came as a bit of a shock to the system." Alex Price remembers leaving with Thornley that day and moaning. "Ooh, the thighs, the thighs," says Price. "Didn't know I even had those muscles."

THE DANCES OF *CURSED CHILD*

· ✳ ·

THROUGHOUT *HARRY POTTER AND THE Cursed Child*, there are several choreographed sequences set to music, which serve to enable a transition between scenes, establish a change in mood or location, or further the story through dance and movement. The play opens with a ballet of suitcases and trunks as wizard families gather, then go through platform nine and three-quarters as they see their children off to Hogwarts. "But Jack Thorne had really set us up a task," says Hoggett, "because the opening section involves Albus's first three years at Hogwarts, written across only twenty-two pages."

In the published script, this is Act One, Scene Four, and is referred to as a "Transition Scene." As the scene shifts quickly between Albus's first, second, and third years at Hogwarts, the characters move through a whirlwind of Sorting ceremonies, Hogwarts classes, and trips on the Hogwarts Express. "It reflects the energy of your school years," says Hoggett. "I'm not sure if I'm particularly unusual, but those years were a blur of events for me, with warring factions that were suddenly harmonious and the messiness that brings. School life for me did feel like a tumble through something."

{ next page }

Sam Clemmett
(Albus Potter)
and the Original
Broadway Company

The three years culminate in a Wand Dance, in which the students—including Albus—are whipped back and forth by their own wands as they struggle to gain control over them and eventually, one by one, manage to cast the *Lumos* spell. After the Wand Dance, Hoggett explains, "wand work becomes much more about the practical." This dance was the place to "blue sky" what wands could do, and explore the emotional side of learning and using magic. "After that moment, it's about the text: whose spell is it, what is the spell, what is the energy behind it, what's happening to the person at the end of it."

Before the first Extraordinary General Meeting of the Ministry of Magic led by Hermione Granger, a dance using cloaks creates the transition from the previous scene of Albus and Scorpius jumping off the Hogwarts Express.

"Theater is all about how you get from moment to moment," says Tiffany. "People call them scene changes, which I think is weird because that sounds like something ends and something begins. The transition from moment to moment is the very fabric of the production." An important difference between theater and film are these very transitions. "Theater doesn't have a jump cut, and that's the joy of it," he continues. "You've got to get that table offstage and that chair on. So, the joy is that you make that the production. Steven and I will storyboard in great detail exactly what the vocabulary of the transitions is going to be."

In this particular case, the Hogwarts Express needs to get offstage, staircases need to move onstage, and a crowd of witches and wizards needs to gather. Hoggett took inspiration for this choreography from patterns of birds in flight, and the result transports the audience from the top of the Hogwarts Express to the Ministry of Magic, bustling with activity.

Staircases appear in Harry Potter's story in different ways. Harry, himself, grew up in the cupboard under the stairs. Hogwarts School of Witchcraft and Wizardry has staircases that move from wall to wall or spiral up to the tops of towers. So, naturally, staircases would play a part in *Harry Potter and the Cursed Child*.

Just as a suitcase could define a train station, and even a train, a staircase can define a home or school, and Christine Jones incorporated stairs into her set design from the start. When Harry Potter returns home from his work at the Ministry of Magic, a lone, long staircase is the only indication of the house's interior. This is where Albus listens in on Harry's conversation with Amos Diggory, and is the hiding place from which Delphini Diggory, Amos's niece, emerges. Staircases form a speaking platform for Minister for Magic Hermione Granger and others at the Ministry. And staircases perform a ballet.

When Albus and Scorpius return from their first trip back in time, Harry decides that Scorpius has been a bad influence and forbids Albus to see him. Following this was a scripted scene between Scorpius and Albus that took place among the moving staircases at the school, with the boys moving around each other, passing each other, becoming farther away from each other. About halfway through the

{ left }

Anthony Boyle
(Scorpius Malfoy)
and Sam Clemmett
(Albus Potter) in
the Original West
End Production

{ next page }

The 2018 West
End Company

rehearsal process, Tiffany and Hoggett went to Jack Thorne with the idea of dropping a line here and there. "Let's try it without that line, and then another line and another, and eventually we just got rid of all the lines," says Tiffany.

Turning and pulling the staircases in the ballet are cloaked "facilitators," as Nuno Silva refers to them. The stairs are configured into L shapes, rotate in circles, brush past each other, part from each other. "The focus is obviously on Albus and Scorpius," says Silva, "and we want the facilitators to be as inconspicuous as possible, but not invisible."

Tiffany also describes it as their way of showing Hogwarts onstage. "We're not trying to hide the people pushing them; we're not saying there's a magical CGI thing about staircases moving, because we all know staircases move around in Hogwarts. But this is also emotional."

The final build of the staircases was achieved in rehearsals. "I don't think when we first created the stairs, we had any idea of how beautifully Steven would choreograph with them," says Jones. "And that is the beauty of

somebody like Steven, who's able to infuse scenery with a soul and with movement in a way that is so special."

Part Two of *Harry Potter and the Cursed Child* opens with a dance that reflects the dark and dangerous world that has resulted from another time turn. The music is heavy and aggressive as witches and wizards in dark, structured cloaks move in quasi-militaristic formations across the stage. Even the cloak work is choreographed with an aggressiveness that defines this alternate world.

The dance also plays with time. Silva explains, "There's the audience's 'real time,' so that they understand what's going on. Then there's a moment, almost like an electric shock, that changes the physicality, that stops or speeds up time." This playing with time via movement would be fine on its own, "but we have the privilege of having Neil's lights and Gareth's sounds," Silva adds, "which just explode the whole thing. The lights and the sounds and the set and other technical elements come together and are interwoven to become something incredible."

There are other instances, not in dance sequences, when time is manipulated. "Most of the movement in the show is about taking time and just letting it stretch a bit deeper," says Hoggett. "It's like seeing something on all sides before you put it back together. You see a bit more than you thought you ever would, and then you return to where you were and carry on, without overstaying your welcome."

• ✳ •

MUSIC

INEXTRICABLE FROM THE MOVEMENT and choreography of *Harry Potter and the Cursed Child* is the music, and from the very start, director John Tiffany and movement director Steven Hoggett had the music of Imogen Heap in mind.

Heap had met Hoggett ten years earlier at Frantic Assembly, when he was directing a new play by Mark Ravenhill called *pool (no water)*. "He wanted me to adapt music from an album I'd just released called *Speak for Yourself*," she says. "It was a unique experience having him specifically ask to extend sections or change the timing of a piece." The Grammy-winning musician's songs had been featured in films and on television, most notably the song "Hide and Seek," from the *Speak for Yourself* album, which has been used in hundreds of iterations, from *The O.C.* to *Saturday Night Live*, to being sampled by Jason Derulo. Hoggett approached Heap about *Cursed Child*, and she was immediately happy to be involved.

Rather than asking Heap to compose an entirely new suite of music for the play, the production drew from her back catalog of instrumentals and the stems of songs. Stem files are a musical track split into four elements: for example, a drums stem, a bass line stem, a melody stem, and a vocal stem. For *Harry Potter and the Cursed Child*, Tiffany estimates that 80 percent was already existing material by Heap. "But they might be different versions that were never released, or stems that we and Gareth Fry could play around with. Then Imogen would build the tracks back up for us."

· ✳ ·

HEAP JOINED THE REST OF THE TEAM at the workshops with her computer, headphones, and various plug-ins. As she watched and worked, Hoggett, Tiffany, or music supervisor and arranger Martin Lowe would pepper her with ideas. "So I'd say, 'I've got stems for that,' or 'I haven't and need to make them.' I'd email my assistant, Alexis Michallek, back in my studio in Havering. I was on chat with him all the time, asking for the stems and if he could send them this way or tempo map them to that," says Heap. "Sometimes I'd have thirty different individual tracks for each song, which would have the different drums, the different strings, all the vocals with which I'd pick and choose what I wanted."

Heap also worked with sound designer Gareth Fry and his team of Peter Malkin and music editor Phij Adams. Heap and Fry could riff off each other, sometimes working with a sound effect, sometimes working with a music cue.

For one scene transition, Fry chose to use the sound of a foghorn. "But he took it to the key of my music from the previous scene," she remembers. "And then I took his sound and brought it into the music." When music needed to match the sound effect of the Hogwarts Express gaining speed along its tracks, Heap took Fry's work and mapped the drums in her music to follow the tempo of the train. It can be challenging to discern where a sound effect ends and music begins, or vice versa.

• ✳ •

HOGGETT AND HEAP'S CHOICES FOR THE music often and unwittingly matched the original theme or lyrics of the piece. "For instance, the music behind the scene with Moaning Myrtle is from an original song called 'Little Bird,' where the lyric goes, 'Little bird, little bird, what do you hear?'" says Heap. "And Moaning Myrtle hears everything in the pipes in the toilets." Another is the use of her song "Aha!" behind the scene of Albus and Scorpius atop the Hogwarts Express, where they're caught by the Trolley Witch. "That's about catching somebody out when they do something that they say they won't do," she adds. Similarly "Lifeline"—the song chosen for the transitional scene across Albus's first three years at Hogwarts—was selected for its rhythm and texture, not its lyrics, and yet it's "about life before and after a moment in your life," says Heap. Rhythm and texture were key in finding the right piece of music for the Wand Dance, Heap's "Cycle Song." "I like the choice of the time signature of the song from Steven's perspective," says Heap. "The students are trying to figure out how to learn wand moves. And the song is a bit awkward—it's not quite in time—so it was really fun to play with."

• ✳ •

MAGIC

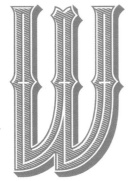

WHAT LIGHT SWITCHES AND GPS are for Muggles, Deluminators and the Marauder's Map are for the wizarding world. Portraits that converse, papers that stack themselves, and traveling through fireplaces is a part of everyday life. The magical illusions performed in the course of the story of *Harry Potter and the Cursed Child* needed to be organic to that culture. "The nature of this show is that it starts with a line of suitcases and the suitcases became a train carriage," says illusion designer Jamie Harrison. "Staircases become bookcases. Arches become forests. The world of magic that we were to create needed to be a part of that world, to feel natural and human and handmade."

Several years earlier, Harrison was invited to be a magic consultant on a production John Tiffany was directing at the West Yorkshire Playhouse. The director had seen his work with Vox Motus, a Scottish theater company Harrison cofounded, which uses elements of illusion, puppetry, and magic effects in their productions. "They're not an add-on of wheeling a box onstage and suddenly we do a trick," he explains. "What we do is create theater that uses magic as narrative." Harrison worked again with Tiffany on *Peter Pan* at the National Theatre of Scotland, and when he heard rumors about Tiffany and a Harry Potter show, he was happy, scared, and amazed when Tiffany called him.

"The opportunity to be the guy who did the magic for Harry Potter? I literally went home and went through the books. Then the worry crept in—what's he going to ask me to do?" Harrison decided that he was not going to hold back anything for fear of failure. "I said to myself, 'You're going to have to be really brave on this project because if we play it safe on Harry Potter, we're never going to make anything different, we're never going to do anything new.' We needed to do things that could excite and create something special." And Harrison did not want to let the fans down.

As they began workshops for the show, Harrison brought on Chris Fisher as illusions associate. Harrison met Fisher during the illusions workshops for *Charlie and the Chocolate Factory* and discovered they had a similar background in magic. "In terms of our job, you can't get much bigger than being asked to do magic for Harry Potter!" Fisher says. "You literally don't get a lot of opportunities like that."

•　✳　•

{ right }

Illusion designer
Jamie Harrison
and set designer
Christine Jones

{ *left* }

Jamie Parker
(Harry Potter) in
the Original West
End Production

{ *next page* }

Nicholas Podany
(Albus Potter)
and Bubba Weiler
(Scorpius Malfoy)
and the 2019
Broadway Company

THE MAGIC OF *HARRY POTTER AND THE Cursed Child* is intricately intertwined with all other departments, and worked specially closely with movement director Steven Hoggett, who always reviewed what the actors were doing during an illusion. "Some of our illusions are really physical," says Fisher. "You wouldn't believe the stretching of the legs, all the contorting of the bodies. Because of his warm-ups, Steven gets the performers ready to do what they need to do." Harrison explains, "For our illusions, actors would often have to do something that would look contrived if it was realized that they were about to do a trick. Steven helped normalize and naturalize these difficult moments."

Collaborations were also key with the other creative teams. "For example, there are specific moments in the show where the costume is vital, but the audience doesn't know this," Harrison explains. "Characters can't suddenly come on wearing a special costume that looks completely out of sync with others in the scene. In order to have that one moment work, we need to feed this costume idea through the whole show."

Often, dozens of prototypes and hours of discussion would pass between Harrison and Katrina Lindsay, or Harrison and Neil Austin or Gary Beestone until a resolution would be found. "There were times when you're thinking, 'I'm never going to make this work,'" says Harrison. "And it would be those times that Katrina or Neil or Gary would say, 'Come on, we're going to get this.' We all knew that we needed to help each other."

• ✳ •

FROM POLYJUICE TRANSFORMATIONS TO Pepper Imps, telephone boxes to the Floo Network, representing the magic of Harry Potter's world was a collaborative effort. Spells and wandwork were no exception.

While the script for *Harry Potter and the Cursed Child* was being written, production assistant Imogen Clare-Wood was asked to make a list of every spell that was used in the play and a description from the books of what each spell looked like. Jack Thorne looked to her for further specifics. "I remember Jack asking if I could give him a list of spells that would be used in a duel," says Clare-Wood. "What they do and what they are so he could figure out what to put in the duel between Harry and Draco."

Thorne used what was possible but also added to the inventory of wizard spells; for example, *Fulgari*, where a wizard's wrists are bound by vicious, luminous cuffs, and *Molliare*, the cushioning charm Albus and Scorpius use when they leap off the Hogwarts Express. These were developed by Thorne, then named by Rowling. "I always tried to name them," says Thorne with a smile, "but she always had something better."

SCOURGIFY!
· ✳ ·

When Hermione visits Harry in his office at the Ministry of Magic, part of the reason, she says, is to check that he's on top of his paperwork. By the papers scattered over his desk, clearly, he's not. To alleviate her dismay at his "chaos," Harry flicks his wand and the papers transform into a neat pile. As the scene was evolving, John Tiffany told Jamie Harrison they needed something for it, and maybe he could do something on the table? "And every time I see it, the audience response is lovely," says Harrison. "It lifts the moment and lets the audience know that they're in a world where anything can happen at any time." Gareth Fry enhanced the sell of the trick by adding a *shhhh* sound as the stacks move. Jack Thorne originally wrote for Harry to incant *Scourgify* when he casts the spell. "Fortunately, one of my nerd mates noticed that's a cleaning spell, not a tidying spell," says Imogen Clare-Wood, though everyone still refers to it as the *Scourgify* moment. "Little things like that, which you don't expect, are a moment of joy," says Sam Clemmett. "They're so well earned. And then we get back to the text and the story that we're telling."

After choosing the spells and naming new ones, the way these spells were cast was an important and heavily examined aspect of staging the show. "The spells in the show are very emotional, personal things," says Hoggett. "And the weight of them becomes more and more significant."

Hoggett, Tiffany, and Jones researched wand choreography online. "They wanted to do it 'properly,'" says Des Kennedy. "But then realized, what's the point of doing that?" Wand style is personal, and since the cast changes year to year, assigning a singular movement to casting a spell didn't feel right. So Hoggett worked with the actors and encouraged them to develop their own wand style.

Sound designer Gareth Fry analyzed each spell and its function within the play in order to create the sounds of spells. "Who's casting that spell? Is it a positive or negative casting of that spell, and are they doing it passionately or gently? Is it more offhand, like *Lumos*, or is it a much more aggressive spell, like a Killing Curse?" Fry looked at the way each actor moved their wand hand to ensure the sound would reflect that movement.

Then he considered the effect of the spell. "Each spell has three components: the person who casts it, the journey of it to the person it's cast upon, and the effect it has on that person, or if it misses," he explains. "So each sound becomes quite complex because you're taking in the character of the person who's casting it, the energy they're doing it with, and then the energy and the impact it has on the target. Each of those had to be tailored very precisely to the performance."

Lighting is also crucial to casting a spell. "We discussed as a team as we worked together about how to do it, about what worked, what was needed," says Austin. In addition to the information they provided, the acknowledged "Muggle" Austin had people on his own team who were very knowledgeable about the Potter world. "So I could ask, 'What color's that spell?' and they could help me out. They could reference back to what's in the books. But we also wanted to use our own imagination, because we are creating a new, theatrical version of it."

THE DUEL

· ✴ ·

ONE OF THE MORE COMPLEX SEQUENCES involving wand work is the duel that takes place between Harry Potter and Draco Malfoy. During Albus and Scorpius's separation, Draco comes to Harry's house to ask that Harry not destroy their sons' friendship. He reminds Harry that he of all people should understand the value of a friend, but Harry is not convinced, and the pair find themselves engaged in a duel in the Potter kitchen.

The team needed to devise ways to create the illusions of Harry Potter twirling through the air—*Flipendo*—or being bounced up and down on the kitchen table—*Mobilicorpus*. Draco is raised and bound with invisible ropes—*Brachiabindo*—and is blindfolded—*Obscuro*.

The battle is choreographed down to the millimeter. "The kitchen fight was the moment that filled me

with the most dread," says lighting designer Neil Austin. When Austin first saw it performed in the bright rehearsal lighting, he assumed that the illusion would be seen in a way similar to the cast members in cloaks who move the staircases. "And Steven was like, 'No.'"

Like many of the illusions in the show, the literal line of demarcation between what the audience sees and how the illusion is being accomplished can be extremely thin. "That's where the fragility of the show is," says Austin, "and that's where the brilliance of the resident directors, and the stage managers and actors, and everyone involved in it comes in." The duel is, however, one of the few illusions that gives the audience a clue of how it's achieved: When Harry casts *Obscuro* on Draco, hands gloved in black velvet appear from the darkness to cover Draco's eyes.

· ✴ ·

{ *right* }

From left,
Paul Thornley
(Ron Weasley),
Noma Dumezweni
(Hermione Granger),
Alex Price
(Draco Malfoy),
Jamie Parker
(Harry Potter),
and Poppy Miller
(Ginny Potter) in
the Original West
End Production

{ *next page* }

Jenny Jules
(Hermione Granger),
Matt Mueller
(Ron Weasley),
Diane Davis
(Ginny Potter),
James Snyder
(Harry Potter),
and Jonno Roberts
(Draco Malfoy) in
the 2019 Broadway
Production

THE TIME-TURNER

• ✳ •

FOR THE EFFECT THAT SIGNIFIES THE use of the Time-Turner by Albus and Scorpius, Tiffany knew he needed a big gesture. "My first idea, which I played with a lot, was a kind of *Wizard of Oz* moment," he explains. "That when we went back, we would either go black and white, but you can't do black and white onstage actually, or go the opposite, so it would be a sepia world." The difficulty and look of each made Tiffany think again. "So, then I explored the Dark Arts," he says with a laugh.

As the characters place their hands around the Time-Turner, clock hands across the proscenium whirl around clock faces, the sound of ticking increases, garbled dialogue floats in and out, and then, suddenly . . .

"There are people who love the fact that they don't know how it's done," says Beestone. "Sometimes, when I've stood at the back, people will tell me their ideas about what it is and they're totally wrong, which is very enjoyable."

Producer Colin Callender came up with the best explanation of the Time-Turner effect, also called the wobble, for his young daughters. "I told them that there are stagehands outside the theater on both sides, and how it happens is that they shake the theater."

The effect of the Time-Turner takes a huge amount of skill from the performers. "They need to really understand the technical side of things," says Harrison, "the technique of how they're doing it, and why it won't work if they deviate." Body placement and positioning is critical to the illusion. "But it should look natural and look simple," says Fisher, "and if it does, that means they're doing their job really well." Add to that expressing the emotion of the character while doing it. "It takes a while for those things to bed down," says Harrison, "which is why we rehearse it from the very, very, very beginning so that they can embody it and it becomes so second nature that the character is allowed to flow. Otherwise it halts actors from being able to deliver the character because suddenly they have to snap out and think, 'Oh, I've got to stand here and do this and do that.'"

• ✳ •

CHAPTER

4

DESIGNING

HOGWARTS

**B**RINGING THE CONTINUED STORY of Harry Potter to the stage introduced a world of questions to be answered by the creative teams handling set design, props, costumes, wigs, hair, and makeup, sound, and lighting. What was Harry and Ginny's home like? How would a spell sound? What would the latest Minister for Magic wear? How would one create a forest, a train, or an owlery onstage?

Design, to set designer Christine Jones, is problem-solving. "From day one, from workshop one, you're given these various equations and you solve them, over and over and over again. It's almost mathematical. If character A needs to appear from lake B and then reappear from lake C, how do you solve it?" If the first way tried doesn't work, another way is tried, and another, until you find the solution.

Speaking to the creative department heads, it's clear that *Cursed Child* was an unusually collaborative project. "It's not like one moment is a costume moment, one moment is a lighting moment, and one moment is a set moment," Jones explains. "Almost every single thing that happens in the show is sound and light and costume and props and magic and direction working together."

Producer Colin Callender adds to that, describing the decision-making behind the realization of the show as organic. "We didn't go into it saying here's what we should do," he explains. "The way everything emerged was a really powerful creative process that grew out of a group of committed, talented people working together in a way that actually brought out the best in all of them."

• ✳ •

{ *right* }

The Original West
End Company

{ *right* }

Set designer
Christine Jones in
the design workshop

SET DESIGN

A S SET DESIGNER CHRISTINE JONES prepared to start working on *Cursed Child*, she revisited the seven novels for inspiration and visual references. "When John Tiffany invited me to be part of the team I was, of course, overjoyed," says Jones. "I was familiar with the books because I have two children, so I had either read or listened to all of them before." But she found herself taking fewer notes during her rereadings than expected. "We think we know exactly what these worlds look like," says Jones, "but in the books J.K. Rowling actually left much up to the imagination. She described the qualities and the emotions of the spaces, but very little visual detail."

For Jones, the minimal description was a real opportunity to use theatrical language to tell the story. "One of the definitions of something 'theatrical' is that it engages an audience's imagination. With books, the author and reader collaborate to create the images in your head; in theater, we collaborate with the audience. And often the things you leave out are as important as the things you show."

Jones knew that the production would be required to reinvent some of the events that had been seen in the films with digital imagery, "but we could do it with theatrical tools," she says. "With rough magic instead of cinematic magic. And that's what theater can do so well."

"We wanted to have a completely different type of experience for the audience where you don't need CGI," adds Brett J. Banakis, now international scenic supervisor. "You won't even think about it; you won't even miss it."

• ✳ •

ON MOST PROJECTS, JONES BEGINS BY combing through the script and finding a poetic phrase that serves as a touchstone for her design approach. In this case, following John Tiffany's idea to open *Harry Potter and the Cursed Child* at King's Cross station, she began by doing research at the Tate Modern's bookstore. "I like to go to bookstores to do research, because libraries are infinitely vast, and in a bookstore that's another kind of distillation." There she came across a magazine article about train stations that featured a quote by the American writer Thomas Wolfe. The quote cites train stations as being one of the few buildings that can hold the sound of time. "And that was the moment where I felt this resonance," says Jones. "They do mark the beginnings and endings of your journeys in both very epic, but also very specific, ways. You can see people on the platform kissing each other good-bye, kissing each other hello. The sense of journeys, the way he describes time as this envelope spoke so specifically to the play. Finding this quote was to me a sign from the theater gods that said, yes, you're on the right path."

Jones and Banakis took advantage of the many train stations in and around London, visiting Paddington, Victoria, St. Pancras, "and, obviously, King's Cross," says Banakis. The challenge was not to re-create King's Cross specifically, but to evoke the sense of the station while also designing a set that could be restaged or relit to create different locations. Built in the Victorian era, King's Cross station sports two eight-hundred-foot-long train sheds topped by barrel-vaulted roofs that rise to over seventy feet. "It's like a giant open window out to the world," says Jones. But it would be difficult to replicate that scale within a theater, so Jones and Banakis started looking at smaller spaces within train stations, and soon found an old

image of the St. Pancras booking office. The room features a large clock on its walls and is a combination of Gothic arches, brick walls, and Tudor-style paneling, a grouping of forms that reflects the timelessness of Hogwarts and the wizarding world. "We knew we could do the show in this room," says Banakis. "This could be the set."

"There was a time when St. Pancras was in disrepair before they renovated it recently, so there were photographs of it in moments that were caught in time," says Jones. "We thought that it would be this room, that it would be somewhat charred and dusty, like a room that hadn't been visited for some time. That became a gold mine of an image." Jones feels that the station seen on stage is a three-dimensional collage of elements from St. Pancras—the clock and the paneling—and the archways from King's Cross. "And we were inspired by visiting train yards to create a turntable like the mechanisms that

"Few buildings are vast enough to hold the sound of time, and now it seemed to [him] that there was a superb fitness in the fact that the one which held it better than all others should be a railroad station. For here, as nowhere else on earth, men were brought together for a moment at the beginning or end of their innumerable journeys, here one saw their greetings and farewells, here, in a single instant, one got the entire picture of human destiny. Men came and went, they passed and vanished, and all were moving through the moments of their lives to death, all made small tickings in the sound of time—but the voice of time remained aloof and unperturbed, a drowsy and eternal murmur below the immense and distant roof."

—THOMAS WOLFE, *YOU CAN'T GO HOME AGAIN*

{ *below* }

The booking office at St. Pancras station (London, 1912)

turn the trains around. We took these elements and made them our own in certain ways. We changed some of the details but also stayed true to the components."

• ✳ •

AS SHE BEGINS HER WORK, JONES'S PRO-cess is to put together a collage of images and impressions. "You want to have a coherent set of influences," she says. "If it's too scattershot, then it lacks integrity. But I think you intuitively gather what you need in the cauldron."

Jones and Banakis printed the images they liked as they researched ideas. "Once you start getting all of these, the idea is to organize them so that they start having a narrative quality of their own," she adds. At the first work shop, they started by taping the images to the walls. "We kept moving them around, rearranging them, and adding more," says Banakis. "At the end of the workshop, we taped all the images together, front and back, and rolled that up to send back to America to start work." By the end of this process, the collage they put together was twenty feet long.

Next Jones puts together a road map of the production in the form of small pictures created with colored Sharpies. "They're like football diagrams," she says. "I use colors and shapes and letters to signify all kinds of different things." The pictures are a way to track through the whole play in a graphic format. "It becomes a shorthand," she says. "This is the train carriage, this is the train start-

ing. This is Sorting, that's Hogwarts. Harry's office, telephone box, home, bedroom, dream, voice. I learn so much from doing this; I learn the rhythm." To anyone else, they might look like doodles, but Jones knows exactly what's happening on the pages, and at some point, these also go up on a wall. "I'm tracking the characters, who's coming, who's going. I'm imagining entrances and exits and levels. It's a way of memorizing the action and imagining what is taking place." As particulars are figured out and decisions made, the sketches become more detailed. "In a way, you're conjuring the mood of the event or room," she explains. "And at the same time, you're conjuring the emotional life of the world."

Simultaneously, Banakis draws his own doodles. "I have a separate little book of doodles where I am technically

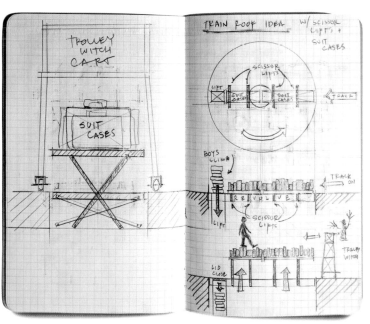

{ above }

Set designer Christine Jones's studio, with set model and inspiration collage for *Cursed Child*

{ below }

Scenic supervisor Brett J. Banakis's notebook

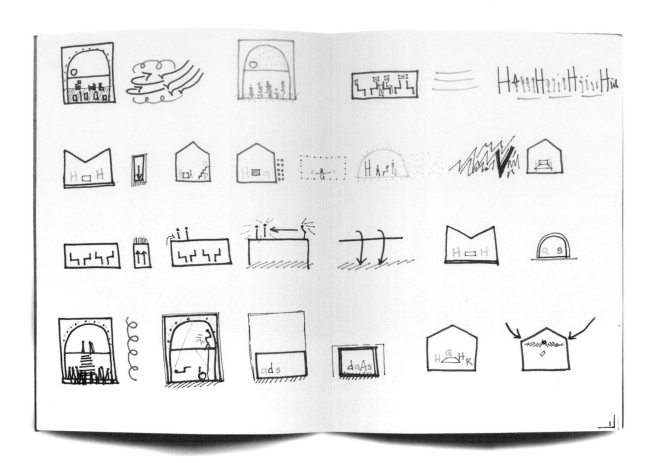

{ *right* }

Select Sharpie
sketches by
Christine Jones,
outlining the
set design for
Cursed Child
scene by scene

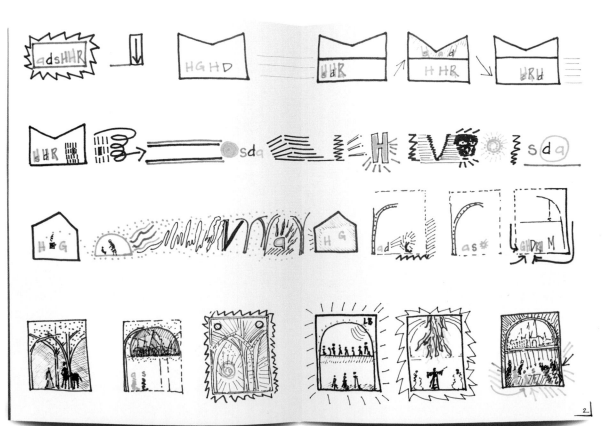

figuring out can we do this or can we do that," says Banakis. "I find that in the spectrum of very technical to the—I want to call it 'finger painting'—we all fall a little bit on either side of center," he explains. "I'm on the more technical side and Christine's more on the finger-painting side. We meet in the middle in a way that's been very fruitful. I would say that we're greater than the sum of our parts."

Jones considers the set itself as its own form of collage. "We collected all kinds of different research, so if you really study the set you can see some of the details from Paddington, some of it's from Victoria, and some of it's from that room in St. Pancras."

• ✳ •

"IT'S ABOUT KNOWING WHAT CAN BE SOLVED THROUGH SET DESIGN, OR WHAT MIGHT BE BETTER HANDLED THROUGH ANOTHER DEPARTMENT."

—CHRISTINE JONES

ONCE THE PROGRESSION OF THE PLAY'S scenes is laid out in Sharpie form, Jones uses it as a template to tackle the tasks before her. "It's as if somebody gave us a series of math equations and said, okay, how are you going to solve these?" says Jones. At times, it's about knowing what can be solved through set design, or what might be better handled through another department. In the very first scene, for example, wizards and witches go through the wall of platform nine and three-quarters. "As a set designer, you think, well, I'm not going to put some fake brick wall on stage in spandex and have people walk through it," she says. "That's just going to be awful. So, I ask myself, what's the before and after; what's really happening?" As Jones saw it, the location doesn't actually change; rather it goes from a world full of Muggles to a world full of witches and wizards. "It's about the people, it's actually not about the set. So, I realized, it's not me, it's a costume idea here!"

• ✳ •

{ left }

Noma Dumezweni
(Hermione Granger),
Paul Thornley
(Ron Weasley),
and Jamie Parker
(Harry Potter) in
the Original West
End Production

{ *above* }

Christine Jones
presents the set
model to the
Cursed Child West
End company and
production team.

{ *below* }

Miniature set
pieces from the
set model box

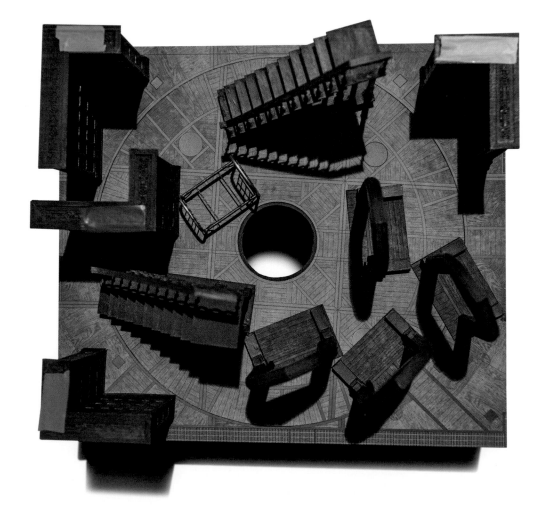

{ left }

Christine Jones,
Brett J. Banakis,
and the design
team constructing
the main set
pieces and dragon
sconces for the
Palace Theatre

{ *right* }

Sam Clemmett
(Albus Potter)
and Jessie Fisher
(Delphi Diggory)
in the Original
Broadway Production

FOR THEIR FIRST TIME TURN, SCORPIUS, Albus, and new character Delphini "Delphi" Diggory travel to the Forbidden Forest at Hogwarts, near where the first task of the Triwizard Tournament was held. The architectural language that Jones had created, with sweeping Gothic arches, lent itself easily to a train station, a thousand-year-old school, and a Ministry environment. "Then we had to think about how to do a forest," says Jones. "And it was just one of those moments where you have a flash of inspiration—what if those arches came apart?" Working with Tiffany, it was decided that a section of each arch would split off. Once they split and move into place, a forest is created, including branches that sit inside the arch sections.

In order to generate the thick density of branches desired for the small amount of available space, three different materials are used. "One is flat cut-out branches out of a material called Sintra," says Banakis, "which is extremely lightweight. There's a heavier, twisty type of wood that's actually called dragon wood. And the smallest branches are birch. The combination of these three layers makes it feel as if it has more to it than it does."

Lights shine upward to give a glow to the bark of the wood, and lights also play at the top of the set, to add to the feel of a forest canopy.

The Forbidden Forest branches found their way into another part of the set when the show moved to Broadway: the maze from the third task of the Triwizard Tournament. For the original production in London, the maze was represented by a series of paneled walls that were choreographed into various positions. "This was something that all along the producers had been saying didn't feel quite as robust or as realized as other gestures in the show," says Jones. "We let that sit with us for a while, and then came back to it, thinking how we could push the idea further."

For New York, the maze walls were constructed from a variation of the same branches used to illustrate the Forbidden Forest. "Once we had the idea to see inside the walls," says Jones, "we could use the same vocabulary for the maze. It's still about the walls coming apart, and you're using elements that you have onstage already." Eventually, the paneled walls used in London were swapped out for the wall of branches. "When we saw no trees and it was paneling only, it felt very heavy," Jones

continues. "You didn't go as deep into the maze and it didn't allow your imagination to go all the way."

Some changes to sets or mechanisms onstage come about because of theaters with different layouts, but some are purely about the show. "Even with as much rehearsal and tech and preview time as we had in London," Jones says, "the more you see something, the more you go, oh, I have one more idea, I have one more idea. And I think that's a very specific example of how theater is a living, breathing sculpture."

• ✳ •

ALBUS AND SCORPIUS TIME-TURN TO the second task of the Triwizard Tournament, which takes place at the lake on the grounds of Hogwarts, where the four champions must retrieve a treasure that has been taken from them and hidden under its waters. They enter the lake through pipes in Moaning Myrtle's bathroom.

"There's just nothing beautiful about a toilet onstage," Jones says. "We tried to do rows of toilets and all kinds of ideas. Then we thought maybe we could create more of a communal sink that you might find in a dorm." Jones asked Jack Thorne and J.K. Rowling about the viability of this idea and got the green light.

• ✳ •

{ below }

Annabel Baldwin (Moaning Myrtle) and Sam Clemmett (Albus Potter) in the Original West End Production

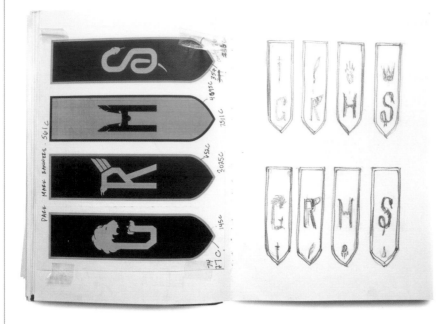

{ *above* }

Original sketches
and Rex Bonomelli's
renderings of the
Hogwarts house
emblems, from
Christine Jones's
notebook

JONES DOES NOT USUALLY DESIGN graphics, but because the Hogwarts House banners are used in the storytelling, she needed to create these emblems. "We set out to create our own versions for the play, asking ourselves, can we add a twist or reinvent this in some way?" She drew rough sketches of the emblems, incorporating each house's symbols: the lion of Gryffindor, the snake of Slytherin, Hufflepuff's badger, and an eagle's head and wing for Ravenclaw. She then consulted with graphic designer Rex Bonomelli, who created the final designs.

Another prominent graphic is the emblem of Hogwarts, which has been incorporated in the auditorium and lobby spaces of the *Cursed Child* theaters. The Hogwarts *H* adorns the curtain when it drops between acts; it's worked into the ornate wallpaper and carpet patterns. As was the case for many elements of the show, the inspiration was drawn from a train station, and much of the set has iron arches riveted together. "Everything we did, we had to create our own identity for, and that metalwork became that for us," says Jones. "When we started to look at Hogwarts, I wanted to imagine it as some kind of metal, give it a steel identity. And in the iron-work at many of the stations," she continues, "you see a half-moon or a star, so we had the idea of stars and moons punched out of iron and detailed with rivets." In the center of the Hogwarts *H* is a star. "The idea of the 'star of Hogwarts' became a resonant symbol for us. That *H* is *our* Hogwarts *H*," says Jones.

Embedded in the front edge of the stage is a quote crafted in brass: *Inlustret Lumine*, which means "let the light shine." The words face the actors. "I often talk about how a set is steel and wood," says Jones, "until you invest it with the love and the spirit of the performers and the characters."

Actress Noma Dumezweni remembers the day the quote was revealed to the actors. "There was a moment we were onstage and she said, 'This is for you,'" Dumezweni recalls. "For me, as an actor, that's one of the most magical things I've ever come across."

• ✳ •

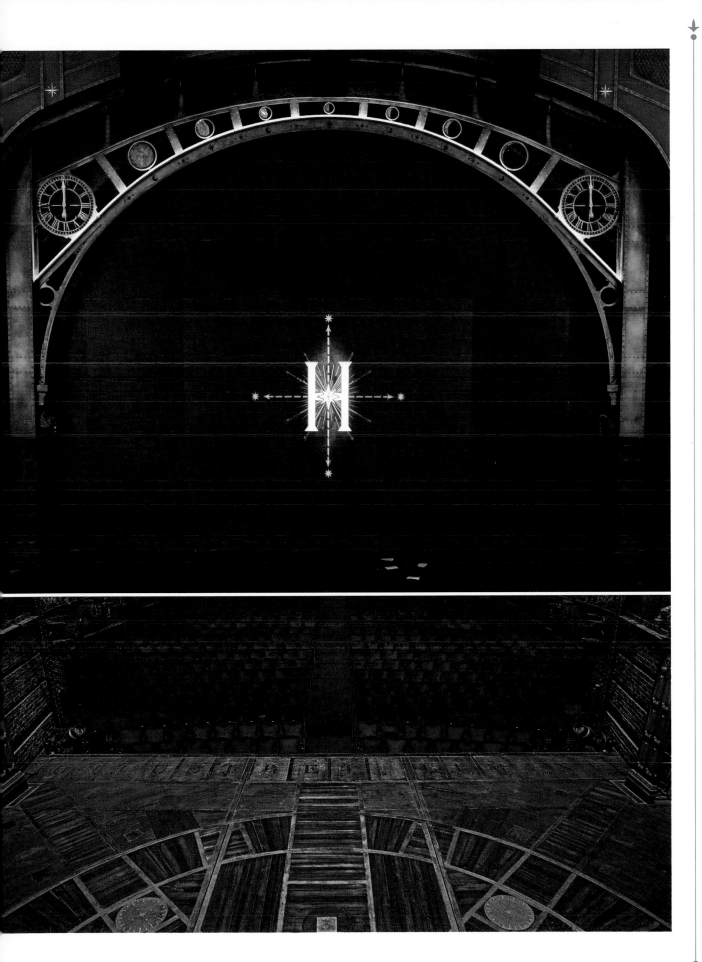

{ *left* }

The Hogwarts *H* projected onto the safety curtain of the Palace Theatre

{ *below* }

Inlustret Lumine, "let the light shine," a message embedded in the stage facing the actors

PROPS

MERICAN-BORN MARY HALLIDAY
and British-born Lisa Buckley, the props super-
visors for *Harry Potter and the Cursed Child*,
were tasked with finding magical herbs and
potions bottles, tables and chairs, owls, and wands.
"Some supervisors are also makers," says Halliday, "whereas Lisa and I are not. We have zero
artistic skills as far as actually making something
with our hands," she adds with a laugh. What
Halliday and Buckley do count among their skills
is finding the right people to provide what they need.
"It's about finding the person who's best suited to do it.
Then we make sure they have the information they
need—all the references and all the materials," Halliday
says. "It's a lot like feeding info to many baby birds."
Buckley explains that one of the most important parts of
their job is having a good address book. "Knowing people and having good relationships is key," she says.

The two women had worked separately or together
on several Sonia Friedman productions, as well as having
worked with Jones and Banakis, so they felt this was a
great opportunity to all work together. Both admit that
they were not as familiar with the Harry Potter story as
others on the creative team. "At the end of the Kennington workshop, I literally asked Brett what a Muggle was,"
says Halliday. "He was like, how are you part of this?
How are you even here?" She also remembers googling
"Moaning Myrtle" during tech rehearsals. "I didn't know
her story," she says. "Who is this woman and why is she
living in the bathroom?"

Halliday and Buckley found many of the pieces
online or at vintage markets or thrift stores. Headmistress McGonagall's desk is from a church. Amos Diggory's
wheelchair was found on eBay. Bespoke props include
papers printed with the Hogwarts and Ministry of
Magic logos.

Buckley feels that a thorough knowledge of the wizarding world wouldn't actually have been an advantage.
"I thought the whole point was for us to react and
respond to what came out of the rehearsal room. I think
it was, personally, better to have come to it without too
many preconceived ideas. If you do, you can't help but
think, oh, that's not how I imagined it. Or, I didn't really
see it like that. But I didn't have any frame of reference,
so it was really helpful."

• ✳ •

{ above }

Harry Potter's
desk at the
Ministry of Magic

{ next page }

Hermione Granger's
desk at the
Ministry of Magic

ANYTHING FROM THE TROLLEY?

• ✳ •

IN TIME-HONORED HOGWARTS EXPRESS tradition, the Trolley Witch pushes a cart filled with treats down the train corridor for students to purchase. Jones asked Halliday and Buckley to come up with their own designs for the sweets, some of which came from the books, and some that were new confectionaries.

"Obviously, there were a few that were very specific and mentioned in the script," says Buckley. Bertie Bott's Every Flavour Beans are on the trolley, along with several Honeydukes specialties: Liquorice Wands, Pepper Imps, Cauldron Cakes, and Peppermint Hum-bugs. "Then we made up a whole load of names, which was great fun." Halliday and Buckley's new sweets include Popping Pixie Wing Dust, Dew Dew Psychodrops (They'll Put a Spell On You), and a new line of carbonated drinks: Bubble Brew (It's Burpalicious!) and Exploda Soda. The props supervisors worked with a graphic designer to come up with fonts and designs, and a cohesive color palette.

The team came up with shapes and textures for the sweets that would provide good visibility for the audience. But the first time they loaded up the trolley, "it looked like a bunch of stuff thrown on a cart," Halliday admits. They realized that the candies needed to be arranged in a more regimented way, like a candy shop itself with designs and tables of offerings.

Another consideration was that anything loaded onto the trolley cart needed to be lightweight. "It has to be lifted up and moved around," says Buckley. "So, we had to keep taking away as much of the weight as we could. And that's harder than it seems." Plastic sweets jars are used, which luckily have the vintage feel they wanted. Other containers are cardboard tubes, empty aluminum cans, and plastic fish bowls. Inside are candies constructed from pom-poms, wadding, packing peanuts, and even hair curlers, sprayed with different colors. "There are polystyrene balls that are 'gilded,' and painted paper balls," says Halliday. Some plastic jars and boxes that are hard to see are actually empty, with an image of candy inserted inside.

• ✳ •

GILLYWEED

While leaving Myrtle's bathroom to travel through the pipes into the lake, Albus and Scorpius eat gillyweed. Halliday and Buckley offered actors Sam Clemmett and Anthony Boyle a smorgasbord of edible possibilities to represent the plant that allows the consumer to gain webbing between their fingers and toes and grow gills to breathe underwater. "They wanted something green, of course," says Halliday. "So, we put together a presentation of things that could work: sliced-up apple skin, actual seaweed and samphire, and liquorice laces. They tried them all, and decided on the apple skin."

THE OWLERY

• ✳ •

WHEN HALLIDAY AND BUCKLEY WERE asked to create an Owlery, they immediately purchased a large book on owl species and gave it to Jones. "She marked up a lot of owls that she particularly liked," says Buckley, "for the way they were sitting, or looked, or had interesting features." Halliday already had cages made, so they knew what sizes the owls should be. "We went to a friend we now call Charlie Owl," Buckley continues, "who I had worked with on a production about Noah's ark, and she started looking at different materials to use." One early take was to create the owls out of paper, and in fact, in addition to brown paper, pages from Harry Potter books were used. The final creation of the owls combines fabrics, feathers, sturdy brown paper, and leather. "We're so sad they only get one scene onstage in the dark," says Halliday. The owls hang above Albus and Scorpius when they meet in the Owlery to make plans. "We knew that nobody would ever see them," Buckley adds, "but it was such a lovely thing to create this flock of those owls. Sometimes, it's actually nice to provide props that nobody really sees, but you know are there."

• ✳ •

{ above }

Assistant stage manager Sally Inch (left) and props supervisor Mary Halliday with cages for the Owlery at Hogwarts

{ inset, at left }

Christine Jones with owl prop in the design workshop

{ left }

Sam Clemmett (Albus Potter) and Anthony Boyle (Scorpius Malfoy) in the Original West End Production

DURING REHEARSALS, JONES WOULD watch each performer and try in some way to channel them to design their wands. "That was such a joy," she remembers. Jones consulted Rowling's novels to be consistent with the wood of each wizard's wand, but the interpretations are hers. Soon enough, batons and drumsticks were exchanged for the real wands.

Buckley and Halliday found a wood-carver who worked out of a shed based near their workshop. "We asked him to find some sticks in the woods and to whittle some for us," says Buckley. "We gave him an idea of the length, and that was pretty much it. He did ten for us, which we took into the rehearsal room." Positive and some not-so-positive reactions were gathered and conveyed back to the carver, who produced a larger second batch.

At the same time, Jones and Tiffany were thinking about what the wands might do. "In the beginning, we were working with a special effects person, trying to figure out if a light came out of the wands," says Jones. "Or, what if you could see a spell in the air, if it develops into a shape that's its intention?"

"There were original thoughts of the wands being very complicated," says Halliday. "But you just can't achieve a delicate wand in something that's covered in LED lights. So it was realized that they had to forfeit those electronic bells and whistles and just go with these very beautifully done whittled sticks."

Halliday and Buckley continued to ask the carver, Jim Smith, to provide his whittled sticks, in addition to the specific "hero character" designs Jones had drawn.

"Apart from the hero wands, there are two types of wands, which are the skinny wands and the wonky wands," Buckley explains. "We'll literally call him up and order thirty-five wonky wands." It wasn't until nearly five hundred wands had been provided that Smith commented that the sticks he was whittling were a lot like wands. "We hadn't told him what they were for, even though he'd signed his nondisclosure agreement," continues Buckley. "We didn't want to put extra pressure on him."

Depending on their use, some wands are created in rubber, but wood is still used for the ensemble. "He uses oak, hawthorn, apple, ash, beech, and sycamore," says Buckley. "Some are a lot easier for him to use than others. We even cut back a tree in our garden and took him some of the branches from that and he used them." The wooden wands are stained or painted to highlight their designs, and usually have a wax or varnish on them for protection. "Some of them take the stain or paint really well, some of them take it differently," Halliday adds, "so they all change and take on a life of their own."

As the show went into its third year, Halliday and Buckley estimated that Smith had carved more than two thousand wands for them, distributed among London, New York, and Australia. "We felt we needed to keep the consistency with the process for the hero wands, because they're the ones that are in the photos, they're the ones that are a bit more prevalent," Halliday explains. "But," adds Buckley, "I think Jim's just really happy sitting in his shed with his knife just whittling away."

Actor Paul Thornley remembers receiving his wand. "When I was handed this, it involves so much love," he says. "If you're sitting anywhere other than the first two rows, you're going to have no idea how much work has gone into that. Hours and hours and hours, and that's Christine Jones. Suddenly, you're in charge of this beautifully crafted thing, and it was a lovely thing to have."

On opening night, every single person who had worked on the show—from the production assistants to J.K. Rowling—received a drawing by Jones or Banakis of a wand designed for them.

● ✳ ●

{ *right* }

Original wand
design sketches by
Christine Jones

HARRY'S WAND
"Harry's wand
evokes the roots of
a tree, symbolizing
his deep connection
to his family, and
arteries that speak
to his place at the
heart of these
stories and to his
renowned golden
heart," explains
Christine Jones.

GINNY'S WAND
"Ginny's wand is
cozy. Like a warm,
soft embrace
that emanates
from a loving and
fierce core."

RON'S WAND
"Ron's wand is like
a striped sweater.
It makes you smile,
it makes you feel
warm and fuzzy.
It comforts you."

HERMIONE'S WAND
"I imagined
Hermione's wand
as a living organ,
full of power and
possibility."

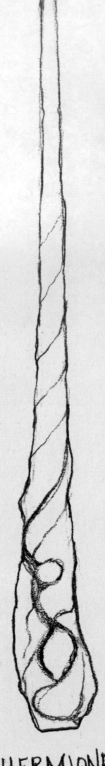

HARRY
VEINS
(HOLLY)

GINNY
COZY

(YEW)

RON
STRIPED

SWEATER

(CHESTNUT)

HERMIONE
(VINE)

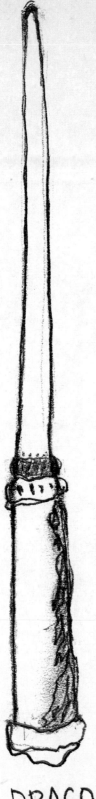

ALBUS'S WAND
"With Albus I was thinking that he's such a worrier," says Jones. "So it's inspired by the buds you see on cherry branches. He could use it as a worry stone to run his fingers on and feel comforted."

SCORPIUS'S WAND
"I thought about how tortured Scorpius is. As an extension of the self, the wand bears the marks of his soul counting the days till he could go to Hogwarts, or perhaps even self harming for relief from his pain."

DRACO'S WAND
"Draco's wand is the most elegant of the wands we created. It embodies his aspirations to be a better parent than his father was. It has pride in its shape and integrity in its core."

ALBUS

KNOTS

(CHERRY)

SCORPIUS

NUMBERS

MARKS

(WILLOW)

DRACO

SABER

(HAWTHORNE)

COSTUMES AND WIGS, HAIR, AND MAKEUP

AS COSTUME DESIGNER KATRINA Lindsay works, she visualizes a sculptural picture and color palette of what will be seen onstage. "When designing anything from the main character looks to the school jumpers, it's like viewing a painting," she explains. With that in mind, Lindsay had a sudden, panicky thought while sketching out the costumes for *Harry Potter and the Cursed Child* in her home studio. "I remember thinking, oh god, everything's going to be black and everything's going to be the same silhouette with the cloaks. How do I make it varied? And," she adds, "how do I achieve that in a way that feels right for this world?"

Prior to her involvement with *Harry Potter and the Cursed Child*, Lindsay won Outer Critics Circle, Drama Desk, and Tony awards for her costume design of *Les Liaisons Dangereuses*, as well as an Olivier Award nomination for *Bend It Like Beckham: The Musical*. Her work spans from theater to opera, ballet to film, where she designs sets as well as costumes, and has done both regularly for the National Theatre.

Working in tandem with Lindsay was Carole Hancock, department head of WHAM, aka Wigs, Hair, and Makeup. The WHAM acronym came about prior to *Cursed Child*, when Hancock was working on the London production of *The Lion King*. "I was so tired of being called the wig lady,"

{ right }

Costume designer
Katrina Lindsay

she recalls. "We're bigger than that." So she and the head of the department came up with the name change, and that's what she's called her department ever since.

Hancock came on the show right before rehearsals began and started brainstorming ideas with Lindsay based on Rowling's books and copious research on both their parts. "There are portrait galleries to visit," says Hancock, "and the internet has heaps of stuff, of course. I've got a plethora of books of period hairstyles and weird fashions. You may not use them, but they're inspiration."

Hancock and Lindsay put together a board of their ideas, not unlike set designer Christine Jones's collage. "We had images of students and teachers, London schoolkids and Scottish schoolkids," says Hancock, describing their thoughts about the contemporary generation, but they also considered the well-established characters from the books. "In a way, we already knew what Dumbledore or Hagrid were like. But Katrina and I worked together on what *we* thought those characters should be and how we would tweak them and change them a little bit."

Designing the costumes and looks for *Harry Potter and the Cursed Child* presented an unusual task: They should be unique to the production, but the audience still needed to recognize each character immediately as soon as he or she stepped onstage. Harry Potter wouldn't

be Harry Potter without his wayward hair, glasses, and lightning scar, but how would he look now as a Ministry worker, frazzled father, and, simply, an adult?

Lindsay strove for a balance of what she felt readers' expectations were and a wizarding world that was recognizable but had evolved in the nineteen years that had passed since Harry's time at Hogwarts ended. "There is a very British, vintage aesthetic that we identify with the world of Harry Potter, and that comes through in the color palette, the materials, and the headwear," she explains. "There is also an atmospheric type of beauty to the world of the play. This world is a mixture of the everyday alongside the magical and more fantastical. And for me, that's the important balance to express. You're not just one thing—you're both."

The design of the costumes evolved from initial sketches to new approaches based on Lindsay's involvement in the show's workshops with the other creative team members, and then rehearsals, consulting with each actor about their character's look. "I felt that my task as a designer was to be true to the physical language happening onstage and the actors who were creating the characters," says Lindsay.

• ✳ •

{ *right* }

Costume fittings
and WHAM sessions,
from year one of
the Original West
End production

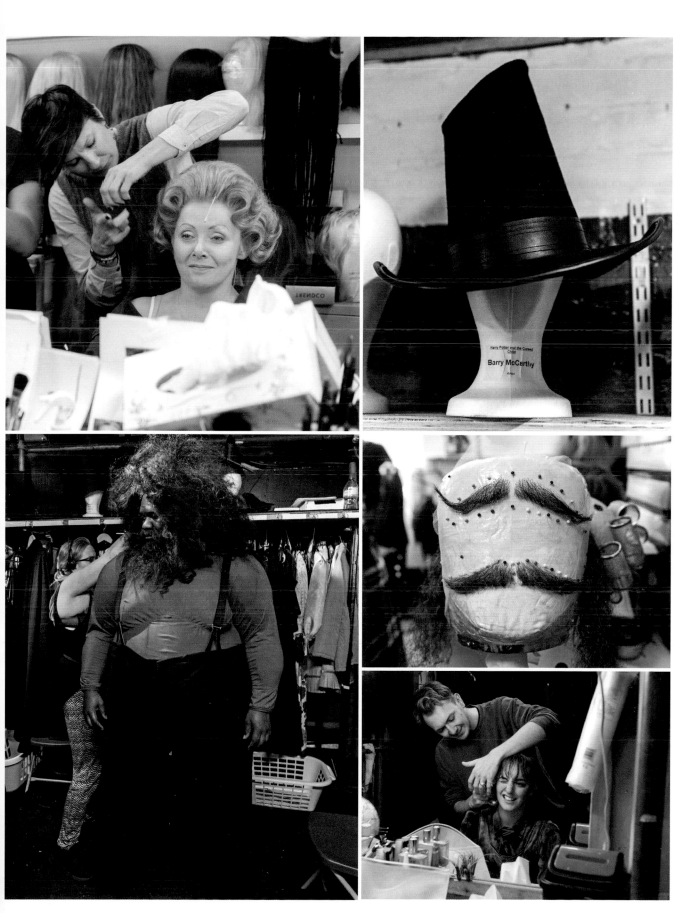

HARRY POTTER

HOGWARTS WILL BE THE MAKING OF YOU, ALBUS.
I PROMISE YOU, THERE IS NOTHING TO
BE FRIGHTENED OF THERE.

—ACT ONE, SCENE TWO

R

Jamie Parker

{ *above* }

Jamie Parker
(Harry Potter) and
Sam Clemmett
(Albus Potter) in
the Original West
End Production

{ *opposite* }

Jamie Parker
(Harry Potter) in
the Original West
End Production

ATRINA LINDSAY AND ACTOR Jamie Parker, who originated the role of Harry Potter onstage, found pinning down the adult Harry's look a surprisingly long undertaking. "It was quite elusive getting there," says Parker. "It's not just a middle-aged civil service suit for him; it had to have something slightly 'ready-to-go action man' about it, but also retain a bit of the boarding school boy. Just being in Chelsea boots or black brogues and an actual fitted three-piece suit looked all kinds of wrong."

"I knew I wanted Harry to have a look that was 'Ministry,'" says Lindsay, "but he would not be comfortable in a business suit. So he *looks* like he's wearing a suit, but it's actually made up of separate trousers, waistcoat, and jacket." Harry wears scuffed-up boots that she describes as combat business shoes. "And his tie is always askew." She felt that Harry would always be happier in the field than at a desk, and wanted to play with that tension.

For Harry's outerwear, Lindsay augmented elements of a trench coat into his wizard's cloak. "I think it's tying in the businessman who's working for the Ministry, for the wizarding world," explains costume design supervisor Sabine Lemaître, who has worked with Lindsay on more than twenty-five productions. "And it was having

something you can relate to in the Muggle world. Trench coats are quite traditional to a British office worker." Lindsay had decided from the start that Harry was not going to be dressed in black, so as part of her character palette, she dressed him in a teal color. "I felt blue was the color for him," says Lindsay, "but I didn't want it to be a very corporate blue." The teal blue also came about from Lindsay's awareness that Harry would need to be visible in the illusions he's involved in. "Jamie Harrison and I didn't talk about Harry having to disappear and stuff like that, but for the phone box trick, for example, it helps that he's in a color—it makes it more surprising when he disappears than if he was too dark and too black."

"What I like about Harry's costume is that on the surface it's simplistic," says Lemaître. "When you watch the show, it's effortless, Harry never changes." Or does he? Yes, he does—Harry actually wears different suits, tailored for specific illusions. "He has four suits and they all do different things," she adds, "but he doesn't *look* like he changes."

The different suits also provide different locations for Harry's wand. "We use wand holsters, we use wand pockets, we have pockets in the trousers," says Lemaître. "But Harry's is particularly like a combat pocket with a flap. He's on the ground, he's in the field. He's like a gunslinger, drawing his weapon." There are three copies of each suit held backstage in case anything happens during a performance.

{ *right* }

Original Harry Potter
costume design
sketches by
Katrina Lindsay

H.P ②

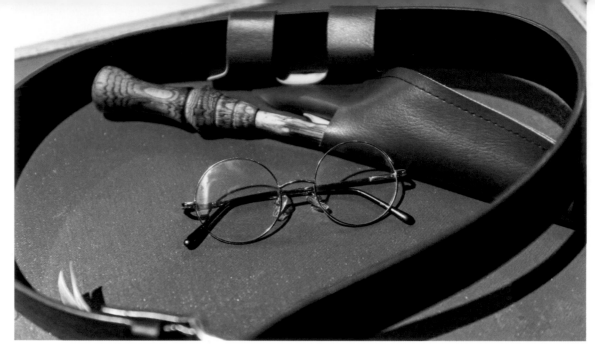

{ *opposite* }

Harry's signature
lightning bolt scar
being applied to
actor Jamie Parker

{ *below* }

The *I Must Not
Tell Lies* scar on
Harry's right hand—
a reminder of
punishment at the
hands of Professor
Umbridge

As for Harry's ubiquitous glasses, he can never be onstage without a pair, so his dresser carries two extra, and stage management also keeps spare pairs on hand. "He could drop them, throw them in the audience, leave them, forget them, or whatever, and it has happened, believe me," says Lemaître. "They've gone all over, especially into the audience, where he's gone *woo-oooh* and they just flew out of his hand. We try to make sure that we really cover ourselves. Harry's glasses are one of the biggest things you have to have near the stage at all times."

The other iconic element to Harry's look is the lightning-bolt–shaped scar on his forehead. Harry's scar is freshly applied before each part, so on days when Part One and Part Two are both performed, it's applied twice. Hancock had a silicone mold made of the lightning bolt, which can be reused. "We have a product called Probondo that's painted onto the mold," explains Hancock. "Then you literally apply it to the skin, peel off the mold, and it's there. It's like a three-dimensional soft rubber." All that's left is to make final makeup touches. The scar is removed easily but has a high tolerance for heat or sweat, so it's not going to slide off Harry's forehead.

The younger version of Harry, seen in his nightmares, also has the scar. "It's hard to see sometimes," says Hancock, "because they have floppy fringes." The year-one cast's young Harrys were able to use the same mold as the adult Harry, except when a child actor with a particularly tiny forehead was cast. "We did need a smaller one, then," she admits, "because the original one filled the area so much, it dominated his forehead." Eventually, the actor grew into the larger-sized scar.

The adult Harry has another scar, not so easily seen from the stage, but all the more important for the actors.

On his right hand is written *I Must Not Tell Lies*. "It's those things," says Hancock, "that you might not know are there, but if you take them away, it gets watered down. All of those things contribute to a look."

It was Parker who requested this scar. "It's important for continuity, and if you don't care about the little things, then pretty soon you find a reason not to care about the bigger things." Parker does reflect gratefully that he didn't have to spend even more time in makeup getting a Slytherin locket scar and some leftover Wormtail and Basilisk scars. "But I also knew that this was a forensic audience and nobody thinks about it until they notice it on a close-up of a production shot or something, and then, 'My god, he's still got the scar on his hand!'"

"You might not be able to see it from the fifth row back," says Hancock, "but he does. The other characters can see it. And it's really important for the fans to have it."

CONSIDER THIS A GENTLE—NUDGE—
FROM THE MINISTER FOR MAGIC.

—ACT ONE, SCENE FIVE

HERMION GRANG

Noma Dumezweni

IN THE ORIGINAL WEST END PRODUCTION

JUST LIKE HARRY, HERMIONE Granger lives in the two worlds of job and home. As Minister for Magic, it was important that Hermione look official, organized, and bureaucratic. "But she's still got that sense of adventure about her. I didn't want her to be stiff." Lindsay's solution was to create a sculptured shape to Hermione's ensemble—jackets that were fitted, nipping in her waistline and giving her an entirely different shape than many of the other witches, as well as a long pleated skirt. "It was about creating a sense of silhouette and structure in the costume that gave her an elegant authority," Lindsay explains. "But it's also about movement, which comes from the pleated skirt and the sweeping trench cloak she sometimes wears."

Hermione's cloak, like many of the others in this production, has cartridge pleating on the back. This method of pleating gathers large amounts of fabric, giving fullness without adding bulk to the garment. It's commonly used to make a skirt more bell-like when attached to a bodice or to give a sleeve more height when attached to a shoulder seam. "Cartridge pleating has a slightly clerical, university feel about it," says Lemaître, and so its use echoes the fullness and sway of the scholarly robes of Hogwarts School of Witchcraft and Wizardry. "We see this pleating repeatedly in the production to understand it's part of their world," says Lindsay. This design repetition works to tie the world together, a subtle visual clue that allows insiders (and outsiders) to recognize their connected culture.

As the production has evolved, Hermione's Ministry outfit has been tweaked slightly from its original design. The front fastenings have changed, and the blouses she wears underneath are sleeveless, for comfort. Little curved pockets have been added to the jacket, into which she sticks her hands ("Very Hermione," says Lindsay). The pockets are also used to hide Hermione's stash of toffee sweets. "I love the bloody pockets," says Noma Dumezweni. "They're much cleaner than an earlier one in the skirt and just make more sense."

Another way of showing Hermione's status, and creating variation in the character's palette, was the color of her outfits. "I remember writing down 'purple' as a Ministry color," Lindsay says. "Quite naturally that became Hermione's key color. The purple is quite regal, brings a sense of authority, and makes her stand out." Hermione also needed to be seen and identified quickly onstage amid the darker palettes of the Ministry witches and wizards.

When Hermione isn't at work, she still retains "that combination of femininity, authority, but also practicality and movement," Lindsay describes. Hermione dons a cardigan with a scalloped neckline and triangle decorations. "I think it's the girl within," says Lemaître. "You've got this official Minister, but the first time she wears this, we see her at the Potter house for dinner. It's a moment just to see Hermione off work, really. She's still the Hermione that everyone knows—she's still soft and feminine."

In the Harry Potter novels, Hermione's hair is described as "bushy." Hancock went over ideas for hairstyles with actress Noma Dumezweni. For events that

{ *opposite* }

Noma Dumezweni (Hermione Granger) and David St. Louis (portrait) in the Original Broadway Production

take place in the present day, at the Ministry of Magic and the Potter house, "it was about containing it and having it practical for her role as Minister."

When time turns and finds Hermione as a (rather severe) Hogwarts professor, her hairstyle changes dramatically, noticeably closer around her head and with a tight braid up the back. In the Dark time turn, Hermione—now known as "Granger" and wanted as part of a small group of anti-Voldemort campaigners—wears a maxi-length purple coat over a black leather jacket, and her hair wild and loose. This third hairstyle is achieved using the same wig as the first style—Hermione the warrior is not so far away from Hermione the Minister as one might think.

Each hairstyle redefines Hermione's silhouette. "As a woman, but I think also as a black woman, our hair has

an important story to tell," says Dumezweni. "It's a silhouette that we want to achieve." When the show went from the West End to Broadway, it was an opportunity for Dumezweni and Hancock "to further explore the possibilities of her hair," says the actress, having liked the changes that had been made for Rakie Ayola, who took over the role in London. As the show grows from London and New York to Australia and San Francisco, the silhouettes will change, but the essence will always be there. "And that's brilliant," says Dumezweni. "It scares me when everything is kept as is from the beginning to the end."

H·G①

HERMIONE:

HOGWARTS IS A BIG PLACE.

RON:

BIG. WONDERFUL. FULL OF FOOD.
I'D GIVE ANYTHING TO BE GOING BACK.

—ACT ONE, SCENE TWO

RON WEASLEY

Paul Thornley

IN THE ORIGINAL WEST END PRODUCTION

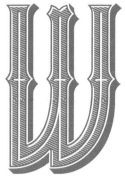

WITH RON, IT WAS ALL ABOUT comfort," says Lindsay. "He's so relaxed and at home in himself, and in the environments he finds himself in. That's what the character felt like to me." Lindsay had also observed actor Paul Thornley, who originated the role in London, in the workshops, as Thornley had participated in them from the start. "And it just felt really right that Ron was this comfortable, very warm character from what Paul was bringing to him. So we went for soft textures—cords and knitwear. And the T-shirt hanging out the bottom, you know. He would never really wear anything too structured." Lindsay definitely felt that Ron wouldn't spend too much time thinking about the style of his clothes.

Respect was always paid to the "Weasley" look—both in the color tones and also the quality of the materials. The Weasleys are known for a very homemade-looking, woolly wardrobe. "I wanted to keep that Weasley family theme with the knitwear," says Lindsay. "I don't think his jumper was homemade by his mum, but I think it has the feeling of something he would go for, having lived in a lot of homemade knitwear in his life. It's slightly too big—it folds softly around his arms and hangs low onto his legs." She does think that perhaps Hermione buys his clothes, so they're more grown-up, "but still with a stripe and orange palette, which echoes his family's look."

"I very much wanted Ron to feel like he'd just got out of bed," says Thornley, who worked with Lindsay and Hancock to develop the look of the character. "Ron is never going to wear anything that's not comfy," he adds. "We had a lot of discussions about that." And is the knitwear comfortable onstage? "The wool's a bit hot, if I'm honest," he admits. "But yes, it is. With those oversized jumpers and that look, he really hasn't changed too much. And he's not doing a job that requires him to look any different."

Ron's orange-and-rust palette also fits in neatly with Lindsay's desire not to have too much black in the show. Not just his clothes, but his hair, will always make Ron stand out onstage. "There were a lot of discussions about exactly how ginger Ron's hair should be," remembers Thornley. Once he was cast as Ron, "No one looked me in the eyes for months. They were all looking at the top of my head, particularly Sonia Friedman. I think Sonia wanted me to look like Beaker from the Muppets at one point, they were trying to have it look that orange!" Different dyes were tried on Thornley's hair, but being a real-life ginger, he came up with the solution that would save him and most future actors in the role from weekly coloring sessions. Thornley made the point to Friedman that red hair typically loses it brightness with age. "I kept finding pictures of middle-aged gingers and showed them to Sonia, saying, 'See?!'" Ron's hair remains true to his age.

While Ron's sweaters are created by a dedicated professional knitter, other items are sourced from retailers or manufacturers. "Our buying department is huge," says Lemaître. "We do source a lot from shoe suppliers, we certainly don't make one hundred percent bespoke footwear." But even shoes bought "over the counter" require attention and adjustment. "Ron's boots, for instance," she explains. "We buy them from the same supplier every year, and then they go straight to our dyers. They get scuffed up and shaded and wrinkled to make them look like his favorite shoes he's owned forever. They go fresh in the box to our dyers, and they come back looking like an absolute state!"

{ opposite }

Original Ron Weasley costume design sketches by Katrina Lindsay

{ left }

Paul Thornley (Ron Weasley) in the Original West End Production

Poppy Miller

IN THE ORIGINAL WEST END PRODUCTION

HARRY. HOW LONG HAS IT BEEN
SINCE YOUR SCAR HURT?

—ACT ONE, SCENE NINE

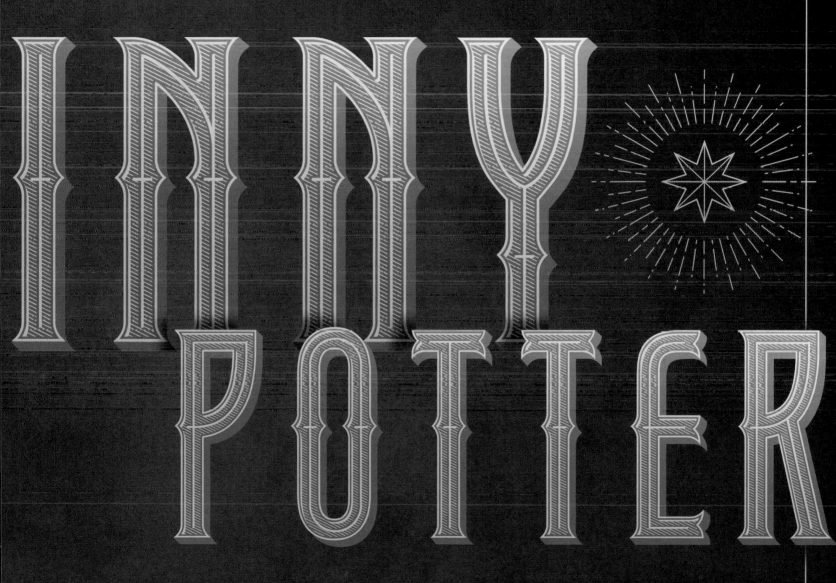

{ *right* }

Poppy Miller (Ginny Potter) with Jamie Parker (Harry Potter) in the Original West End Production

{ *opposite* }

Original Ginny Potter costume design sketches by Katrina Lindsay

CTRESS POPPY MILLER, WHO originated the role of Ginny Potter, remembers her first costume meeting with Tiffany and Lindsay, and seeing a drawing of her character wearing an A-line skirt and simple top, which pleased her immensely. "I thought I was going to be wearing a tracksuit," she told them. "And they both looked at me like, why would you ever wear a tracksuit? Well, because she's the sports editor of the *Daily Prophet*!"

True to Weasley family tradition, Ginny Potter's costumes are a combination of purchased and "homemade." Ginny's sweaters are custom-made by a professional knitter. Her pajamas are sourced, purchased at one of several pajama companies the production uses. "Originally, Ginny's dressing gown was a vintage piece that I found," says Lindsay. "I loved the color and delicacy to it—I saw that as a 'Ginny' thing—it just felt right for her." But because it was a one-of-a-kind item, the only way to re-create it was to print it themselves. Says Lindsay, "We

got into a whole other level of manufacturing and making, which was quite interesting."

Ginny's outfit, unlike many of the other characters', stays essentially the same: a sweater over a simple pleated skirt, with or without a warm coat. At first, she did have more than one costume, but Tiffany pulled back on that. "Quite rightly, he said Ginny needs to wear the same thing because she's always Ginny," Miller explains. "When we're in the different realities, she needs to be the same."

The tones of Ginny's color palette, in light turquoises and sea greens, complement Harry's teal robes more than the warm shades of Weasley wear. "I just felt that it was feminine, and I also thought that it was a nice color against her red hair," Lindsay explains. "It's all about how you make a family work together."

G.P①

Sam Clemmett

A

LBUS
POTTER

S THE STORY OF *HARRY POTTER and the Cursed Child* begins, we meet Albus Potter with his family at platform nine and three-quarters before his first year at Hogwarts, which means he's eleven years old. Albus is played by a single actor in the play, going from a shy boy to a confident (eventually) fourth-year.

Lindsay wanted Albus to appear young and a bit vulnerable in his first year and played around with the idea of the uniforms having short trousers, resembling knickerbockers, "but it just felt too period," she remembers. Actor Sam Clemmett came in with the idea that Albus wears his older brother James's clothing. Clemmett figured that hand-me-down clothes were common for the Weasleys, the family that Harry Potter joined. "His clothes are just a little bit too big for him; he's got much bigger trousers, the sleeves are too long for him," says Clemmett. "I just wanted them to feel a bit heavy and a bit bulky, so there's this constant burden on him that, at the beginning of the story, he can never feel like he can be his own person." As Albus's journey continues, "there's a very subtle change in his school uniform," says Lindsay. "He starts off wearing trousers that are bigger, but for Part Two, they're slimmer and they fit him. It's really subtle and you shouldn't notice it that much. But he grows, he changes."

A slight shift in color also signals maturity: Albus starts off in a pair of light gray trousers but wears a darker shade of gray later in the play. "It's a minor change, but just having a darker leg instantly makes him feel like a senior, rather than junior," Lemaître adds. "I think he gets more self-aware, especially after he meets Delphi Diggory."

Albus's hair gives a small nod to Harry's well-known tousled thatch. "Fortunately, Sam Clemmett had that kind of hair anyway," says Hancock. Lindsay also gave a nod to Harry in Albus's "at home" clothing. "I wanted it to relate delicately to Harry, at least color-wise," says Lindsay. "There's a bluish quality in many pieces, like his stripy blue top and his pajamas." The hoodie Albus wears is another nod to Harry's youthful adventures.

{ left }

Sam Clemmett
(center, Albus
Potter), with
Edward Hyland
(left, Amos
Diggory) and
Anthony Boyle
(right, Scorpius
Malfoy) in the
Original Broadway
Production

A.P ③.

{ left }

Original Albus
Potter costume
design sketches by
Katrina Lindsay

A.P - ①

S

ALL I EVER WANTED TO DO WAS GO TO HOGWARTS AND HAVE
A MATE TO GET UP TO MAYHEM WITH. JUST LIKE HARRY POTTER.
AND I GOT HIS SON. HOW CRAZILY FORTUNATE IS THAT.

—ACT TWO, SCENE SIX

SCORPIUS MALFOY

THE MALFOY LINEAGE IS EASILY recognizable in Scorpius, with his crown of white-blond hair. "There's no hiding with that hair," says Anthony Boyle, the original Scorpius. Certainly, it helps him "pop" among the Hogwarts students, who all wear the same robes, albeit with their house colors added after they're sorted. With that in mind, attention was paid to the clothes worn underneath. Young Albus appears scruffy and rumpled at first, wearing hand-me-downs, but Scorpius, being a Malfoy, is clean and pressed.

Boyle worked closely with Lindsay on Scorpius's clothes. "I wanted thin trousers, almost skinny jeans, to give him this gangly, awkward feeling," says Boyle. "And I didn't want him to have trainers or runners to feel agile. I wanted something clunky and uncomfortable for him to always feel a bit out of place." After two and a half years in the role, Boyle wishes he'd made a different choice. "I'm jumping up and down on a train every night! So I wish I'd have just had trainers on."

The normally dark-haired actor assumed that he'd have to dye his hair for the role, but instead he was told it would be a wig. Boyle asked if he could at least try dying his hair. "They said no," Boyle recalls. "Because my hair is so dark, I would go bald. They didn't want to have a bald fourteen-year-old."

"It's a very, very hardworking wig," Hancock explains. "There are two of them, in fact—a wet wig and a dry wig." Scorpius's wigs are made from *épiler* hair, which is unprocessed and obtained by taking naturally gray hair and pulling out only the white hairs to use. "It's very difficult to get that color hair. Normally you have to process hair to get that color, but processed hair would get too damaged when Scorpius goes into the water—which is chlorinated—so we needed to use unprocessed hair. It's probably the most expensive wig on the stage."

When Scorpius lands in the Dark time turn, his costume changes significantly. Overall, Lindsay wanted to give the wizards in this turn a militaristic look, aggressive and structured. And as this time is very Slytherin influenced, she looked at snakes and snakeskins for ideas. The collar of the students' clothes mimics the "hooding" behavior of a cobra, and the overcoat is split into two little tails. Tech rehearsals necessitated a second coat for Scorpius, when they realized he would be in and out of water. "The coat was wool, so water would have wrecked it," says Lindsay. So the exact same coat was cut out of neoprene. "It's the same black and the right weight to keep the sculptural shape."

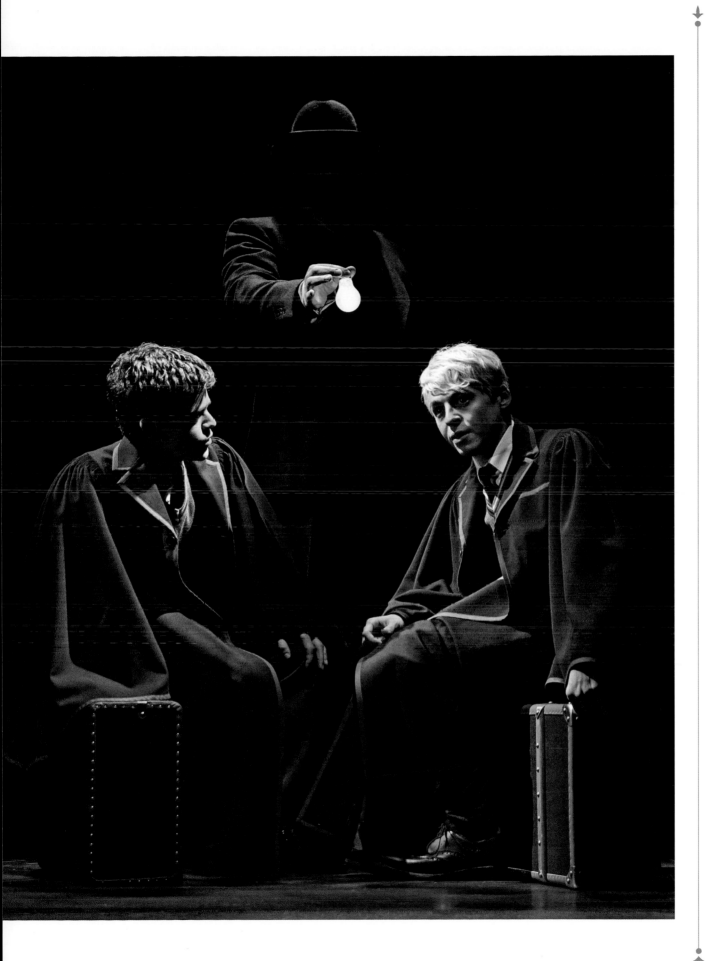

{ left }

From left,
Sam Clemmett
(Albus Potter),
Brian Abraham
(Sorting Hat), and
Anthony Boyle
(Scorpius Malfoy)
in the Original
Broadway
Production

{ *right* }

Anthony Boyle
(Scorpius Malfoy) in
the Original West
End Production

{ *opposite* }

Original Scorpius
Malfoy costume
design sketches by
Katrina Lindsay

S.H ②

Alex Price

IN THE ORIGINAL WEST END PRODUCTION

DRACO MALFOY

I DON'T CARE WHAT YOU DID OR WHO
YOU SAVED, YOU ARE A CONSTANT CURSE
ON MY FAMILY, HARRY POTTER.

—ACT ONE, SCENE SEVENTEEN

{ *above* }

Alex Price (Draco Malfoy) in the Original West End Production

{ *opposite* }

Original Draco Malfoy costume design sketch by Katrina Lindsay

I T SHOULD BE NO SURPRISE THAT Lindsay's thoughts about Draco Malfoy's wardrobe should turn to that of his father, Lucius. "It's just the idea that you grow into your parents in some ways," Lindsay explains. "I was thinking about that a lot while I was working." But as with Hermione, Draco's costume gave the designer a chance to create a silhouette that was its own.

Lindsay started by looking at the fashions of several time periods and was caught by the idea of using a frock coat as part of his outfit. "I put pleating into it, again, because by this point, I knew that it would create this language of movement that I wanted. But Draco's costume is all about formality, so it's also quite structured at the back, with belting. And even where the pleating is there are little tabs as well, so the pleating kicks through in places." A waistcoat tops it all, to gain another level of structure.

Draco Malfoy proudly wears the white hair that marks his family, but has given it his own flair. At first, the hair was long and unbound. "But the first time I walked onstage at a tech rehearsal," recalls Alex Price, who originated Draco in London, "John Tiffany came running up, saying, 'No, no, no, too much like Daddy, too much like Daddy!'" Having it short would be too much like Scorpius's, so Lindsay and Hancock batted ideas back and forth until they decided a new direction for a

Malfoy would be braiding it. "And of course that's exactly right," says Price. "He wouldn't have wanted to look like his father at all." The decision was encouraged and approved by Tiffany. "John likes us to see people's faces," says Hancock, "so that's why a lot of hair is back, like Draco's." Only in the Dark time turn is Draco's hair styled long and loose. "We brought it out then to relate it back to his Death Eater father," says Lindsay.

While Draco's clothes seem rather stern and austere, he wears a number of rings. "That came from Alex," says Lindsay. "To me, jewelry projects wealth," says Price, and perhaps that's one shared trait that can be attributed to the character's father. He started with a signet ring. "I thought it's a very public school thing back in England to have a signet ring," Price explains. "So I brought one in, but it was too Muggle." More "wizardy" rings were found, to the point where he wore a ring on every finger, which proved to be a bit too much. "The ones that remained are angular or Gothic looking," says Price, "all the things that color a Malfoy and a Slytherin."

"We buy lots of different pieces of jewelry," says Lemaître, "and mix them up in a little bag to hand to each new Draco." Lemaître appreciates that the jewelry plays a central part in Draco's costume and that each actor's choice is individual and different, with one exception: the gold band that is Malfoy's wedding ring.

{ *right* }
Alex Price
(Draco Malfoy)
and Esther Smith
(Delphi Diggory)
in the WHAM room
pre-performance at
the Palace Theatre

CLOAKS

• ✳ •

NOT SURPRISINGLY, DIFFERENT CLOAKS are used in the show for different purposes, so though they are all cut from the same pattern, they are created with various weights of wool. "Although they're very simple garments, the weight and the fullness took a long time to decide," Lindsay explains. Once the correct cut was designed, the cloaks are fitted for each actor's height. "But when I was plotting out the number of costumes needed, and how certain things were done, I thought it would be good to have two separate parts to it," says Lindsay. A hooded cape was added that could be worn with or without the hood, which allowed for greater flexibility, especially for members of the ensemble who play a number of roles. "In the Ministry of Magic, they use them without the hoods," Lindsay explains, "and a lot of the time for scene changes they've got the hoods on." For the first cast's performances at the Palace Theatre, over 1,700 feet of wool was used for the cloaks.

Most important was finding what would make the best *swoosh*, and that took some time. The final version of the cloaks didn't arrive until the technical rehearsals were held in the theater, and so the cast was still making do with what they had. "I remember being in a rehearsal room without the right cloaks and they were quite clunky," says movement director Steven Hoggett. "As they did their moves, I found myself making really elegant *whooo* noises, like swishy noises, trying to convince myself that that's what they'd look like. I was also thinking, I'm a man in my forties making *whooo* sound effects in a rehearsal room." As happened so often, Lindsay was right by Hoggett's side as the sequence was being rehearsed, "But I don't *think* she heard my swishing."

DRESSING HOGWARTS

• ✳ •

WHEN KATRINA LINDSAY STARTED sketching ideas for the Hogwarts school uniforms, she wondered if there should be different robes for different school years. "What is the first-year's robe? Should sixth-years be in shorter robes? Is there a ceremonial robe that goes over other robes? A prefect's robe? Do they need a travel robe?" Lindsay asked herself. Eventually, in addition to creating the stage pictures she desired, practicality would influence her designs. "The nature of the show, actually, is that it's really quick and really fluid, so the costumes had to have that same kind of ease and fluidity about them." During the rehearsal period, this approach helped to finalize the clothes, especially when it came to actors playing multiple roles. "Actors needed to be able to move from being a school kid into a Ministry person, then up to a dementor really fluidly," she explains. "That's when I made the Hogwarts uniform a bit more standard."

Once the students are sorted into their houses, hoods lined in their house colors are attached to the basic fitted blazers, "which we call blazer cloaks, of course," says Sabine Lemaître. "They're a school blazer, so they've got collars and lapels and they look like a blazer at the front, but they've got wizardy sleeves. And at the back it's like a cloak." Students also have a choice of separates, such as long-sleeved sweaters or sweater vests, lined with house colors.

The robes have a custom silhouette, with cartridge pleating on the back. "All the fullness in both the pupils'

{ left }

The Original West
End Company

and the teachers' costumes is at the back," says Lemaître. "So, when they run or turn, it creates a *whoosh*, without them even having to manipulate the robe."

The robes are weighted at certain places depending on the material used, to achieve the proper effect with both light and heavy fabrics. And there's a little trick to ensure that the cloaks don't fly off the actors. "They're anchored on with big elastic straps that go under their arms so that they can run around without it falling off their shoulders," reveals Lemaître. "There are lots of little details we do inside to just pull everything into the right place."

The next challenge was to create individuality and the personality of each student under the robes they wore. "For the boys, for example, Karl Jenkins is quite trendy, and he wears skinny jeans and trainers," says Lemaître. "Yann Fredericks is very slender and a bit snobbish. He's very neat, and a bit like Scorpius. Craig Bowker is quite lovable and cute, and he's got baggy trousers and shoes that were clearly bought by his mum."

• ✴ •

THE SORTING HAT

· ✳ ·

DURING THE WORKSHOP PERIOD,
Tiffany and Lindsay discussed what the possibilities for
the Sorting Hat could be, as it would be a talking *and*
walking character in the show. "It was clear from the
beginning that John wanted the Sorting Hat to feel as if
he was taking us through the story, that he was part of
the storytelling," says Lindsay. Tiffany told Lindsay that
he saw the Hat "like a doctor from the thirties or forties,"
she explains, "and even suggested that he carry a doctor's bag." Tiffany also felt that the look of the hat should
be quintessentially British and not a "wizardy" hat. "So I
was looking at hats that felt everyday, though not a
bowler hat nor a trilby," says Lindsay. "A homburg felt
like just the right thing."

The chosen material for the hat is a dark chocolate
brown with a deep pile of peach wool felt that has a light
reflective quality. In the spotlight, it glows.

· ✳ ·

{ *previous page* }

Brian Abraham
(Sorting Hat) in the
Original Broadway
Production

{ *right* }

Original Albus
Dumbledore
costume design
sketch by
Katrina Lindsay

ALBUS DUMBLEDORE

• ✳ •

LINDSAY FELT THAT THE DESCRIPTIONS of Dumbledore from the Harry Potter novels gave her excellent guidance as to how the former headmaster, known to be a clotheshorse, would dress. The challenge to her and Hancock was what to do about the beard? "Originally, we were going to make it very long and have it go over his shoulder," says Hancock. "But when we saw it onstage it didn't really work for the character. We thought about tying it, but didn't like that either." They realized that the simplicity of just having the long white beard flow down in front of his elaborate robes was the look they desired. As the late headmaster mainly appears in portraits, another consideration was what to do when the beard would hang below the picture frame. "So, we tuck it into his costume for the smaller frame seen in Part One," says Hancock. For Part Two, the frame is nearly full-length, so no adjustments are necessary.

{ left }

Barry McCarthy
(Albus Dumbledore)
and Jamie Parker
(Harry Potter) in
the Original West
End Production

{ *right* }

Sandy McDade
(Minerva McGonagall)
in the Original West
End Production

{ left }

Original Minerva
McGonagall
costume design
sketch by Katrina
Lindsay

PROFESSOR McGONAGALL

• ✳ •

PROFESSOR MINERVA McGONAGALL, headmistress of Hogwarts in Albus's and Scorpius's years, is simply timeless. But she is definitely a product of her own past. "I went down the whole Scottish route with McGonagall," admits Lindsay. McGonagall's outfit features the Black Watch tartan, which has a strong green element to it, created in a textured dupioni silk. "The dress is made up of two parts," says Lemaître. "There's a bodice and a pleated skirt, so it does slightly reference a kilt." There's also a surcoat, made from an emerald silk velvet, this time with knife pleats. "So it still ties in with everybody else," she adds. The costume recalls styles of the Edwardian period. "It's not literal, but she's a Scottish authority and she runs a tight ship," explains Lemaître. "I think there's something about the Edwardian shapes of ladies of that time that was about keeping up appearances and being all buttoned up, so those silhouettes lent themselves to McGonagall's characterization."

RUBEUS HAGRID

· ✱ ·

AS THE BELOVED HALF GIANT RUBEUS Hagrid is the Keeper of the Keys and Grounds for Hogwarts, Lindsay knew that said keys would hang from his coat's large belt. "The big belt helps define his shape, but I wanted him to have 'animal' things near him in some way, so we spent ages making talisman-like items that he hangs around himself." Other bits and bobs include a soft leathery pouch; a rabbit's foot; and seedpods. Lindsay also felt that Hagrid would have made the coat himself. "It's based on a traveling coat, with a shawl collar, but all the pockets are different, they're all different fabrics and different sizes. And he probably still continues to work on it." None of the seams are straight and the edges of fabric and leather are raw. Hagrid's hair, a combination of human and yak hair, needed to have height, which is helped out by its wild spidery tendrils.

{ *right* }

Original Moaning
Myrtle costume
design sketch by
Katrina Lindsay

MOANING MYRTLE

• ✴ •

IN A THEATRICAL PRODUCTION WHERE battles are fought with wands and office papers stack themselves neatly, dressing a ghost would seem an easy task. "I wanted Myrtle to feel as if she were in a different time, of course," says Lindsay. "But how do I make her feel as if she's come out of a watery drainpipe as well as being a ghost? How was I to do that onstage?" An old-fashioned pleated school uniform was designed and constructed out of a wavy, fluttery satin silk with stretch for strength, as she is quite physical while spinning on her dais of pipes. "Our dyers create a marbling effect on the fabric that really mimics it being water-stained," says Lemaître.

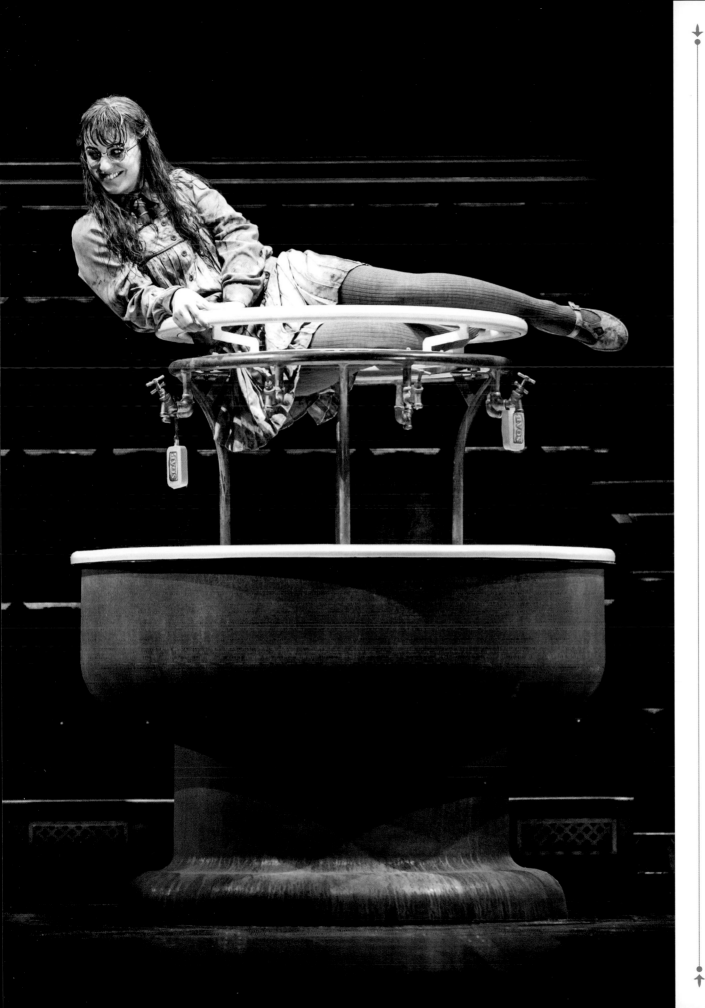

{ *left* }

Annabel Baldwin
(Moaning Myrtle)
in the Original
West End Production

{ left }

St. Oswald's Home
for Old Witches
and Wizards, 2018
West End Production

{ next page }

James Snyder
(Harry Potter) and
James Brown III
(Bane) in the
2019 Broadway
Production

{ *right* }

Paul Bentall
(Severus Snape) in
the Original West
End Production

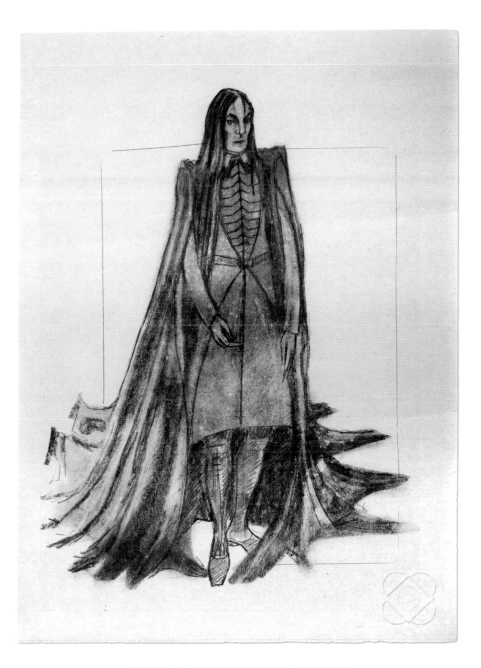

{ left }

Original Severus
Snape costume
design sketch by
Katrina Lindsay

THE DARK TIME TURN

• ✳ •

FOR THE DARK TIME TURN, LINDSAY created what might be called a Slytherin army, influenced by the patterns and banding on snakes. "Or, rather, shed snakeskins," she says. Reptilian-style robes and coats were created out of a black monofiber. "It's got fullness, it's got drape, it crushes into nothing, it's fantastic for choreography, and it lights well," says Lemaître. "It's a true black and finding that is hard." Twisted leather "spines" are laid over a green chest lining, "which not only references Slytherin, but also the dementors' rib cages," she adds. The coat has a forked tail, and the robe's sleeves are split. Hairstyles for the characters who live in this almost martial world are sharp and clean. "Not really like a military haircut," says Hancock, "but everyone looks the same."

Professor Severus Snape, of the greasy black hair and piercing black eyes, is a key character in the Dark time turn. Beneath his split-sleeve black robes and leather frock coats are rows of black leather twists that convey the effect of the braiding on a Napoleonic military jacket.

A PINK-GARBED DOLORES UMBRIDGE appears in the Dark time turn, girlish grin in tow. Lindsay wanted her to seem powerful and majestic, "so I gave her a gown with a university feel, but also with a Tudor slant." Her hot-magenta robes are edged with fur; her cuffs are layers of lace. Her hair is fashioned in the iconic poufy style of former prime minister Margaret Thatcher.

The Harry Potter novels had Umbridge wearing bows in her hair, which Lindsay and Hancock considered, but thought would be too cartoonish. "She was already quite frilly," Lindsay explains, and they recognized that it was twenty-two years since we last saw her. However, she does sport a small bow at the hem of her skirt, and a pussy bow at the collar of her shirt.

{ *left* }

Helena Lymbery
(Dolores Umbridge)
in the Original West
End Production

THE DEMENTORS' COSTUMES, MADE from the super-fine organza Lindsay had carried in her handbag for years, combines two colors of the material. "One is black, the other gray," she explains, "because I just wanted to mix the colors. But the way it's cut, there is a lot of fabric that comes together." The material, which comes from one specific manufacturer in Japan, can only be cut with a hot knife.

The costumes flow at least eight to ten feet below the actors'—or more specifically, fliers'—height. "When we knew which members of the cast would be playing them, I wanted to make sure they didn't look like there was a person in there," says Lindsay. The dementors are a buildup of layers: first, a black body stocking, then a skeletal structure that gives the impression of bony shoulders and arms, and long, skeletal hands. A cone-shaped skirt hides the legs and feet, and what Lindsay calls a "dementor shroud" goes over all. The fliers also wear hoods, veils, and masks.

The masks are 3-D–printed from a scan of each flier's face. "It fits so securely on them because it's their face," Lindsay explains. "It's comfortable; you don't have to re-pad it." One of the benefits of using this new technology is that if there's any wear or tear on the masks, they can be reprinted quickly and exactly.

• ✳ •

{ left }

Costume designer
Katrina Lindsay
outfitting one of
the dementors

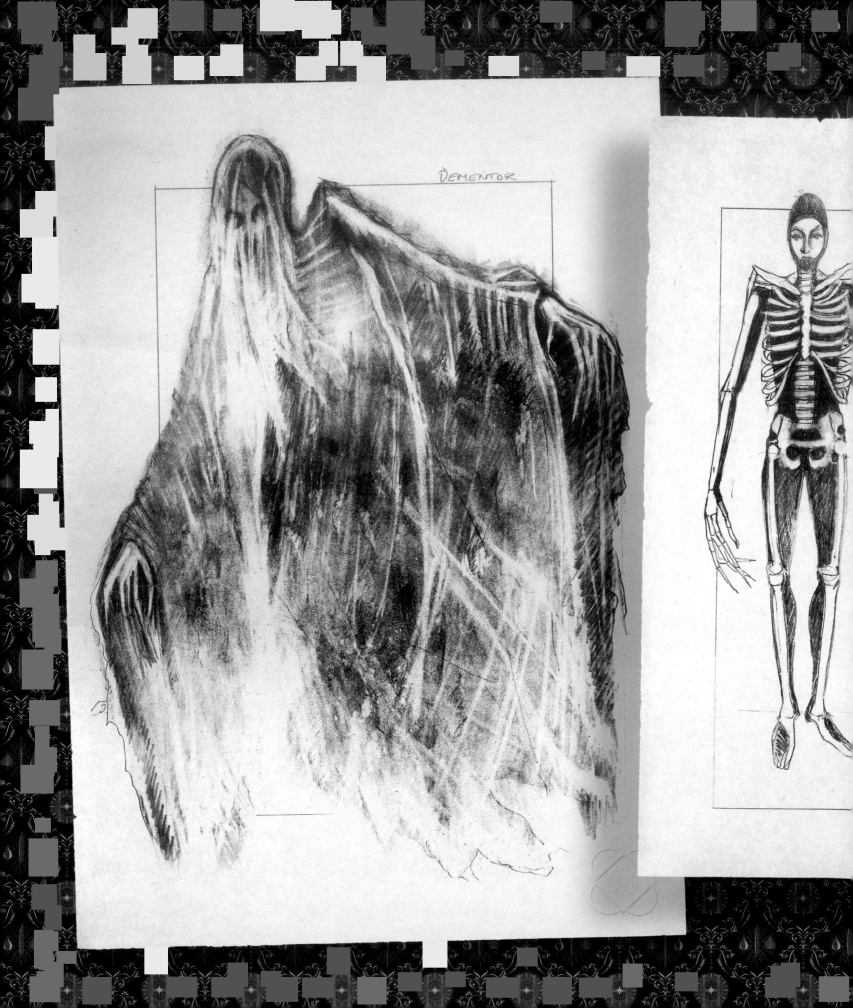

DEMENTOR

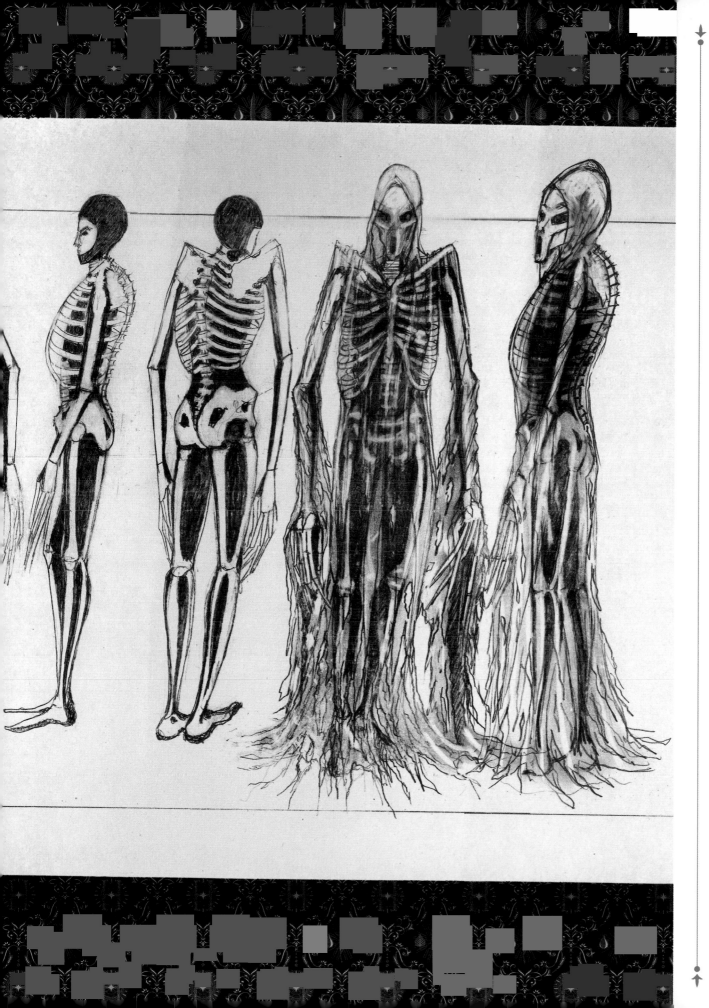

{ left }

Original dementor
costume design
sketches by
Katrina Lindsay

SOUND

SOUND DESIGNER GARETH FRY ORIG-
inally trained as a recording engineer but ultimately decided it wasn't quite the medium for
him. "Then, by chance more than anything, I
worked on a production of *Amadeus* and fell in
love with the liveness and the connection that the
music and the language had with the audience."
Sound, he explains, has functional aspects such as
making voices louder or setting time and location,
but "it's also where so much of the emotional
aspect of a show is conveyed."

Fry's association with director John Tiffany began
with *Black Watch* in 2009 at the National Theatre of
Scotland, for which he won his second Olivier Award,
for Best Sound Design. They continued working
together at the National on *Be Near Me*, *Peter Pan*, *The
Missing*, and *Let the Right One In*. For the latter, he won
the 2015 Drama Desk Award for Outstanding Sound
Design in a Play. Having such a long history with a specific director generates a shared, and sometimes an
even silent, vocabulary in discussions about the play
and its needs. "Because we've worked together for so
long, a lot of the time John just lets me get on with it,"
says Fry. "He'll give me a raised eyebrow if there's
something he doesn't like, and I'll go, okay, I'll change
that, then."

• ✳ •

"THERE ARE ABOUT TWO THOUSAND
individual sound cues in the show, and possibly only
three of those are naturalistic sound effects; everything
else is magical in some way," Fry says. "You can't type
Expelliarmus into a sound effects database and get a
sound to come up in the same way you can type in taxi or
plane. So everything had to be created from scratch and
from imagination. And everything makes a sound."

Developing the Parseltongue that's spoken in the
play took him a bit of time. "It was just tricky to find the

right balance of snakiness and human voice. But that was
a really fun one to do." The snakiness eventually came
from software he developed.

At times, sounds were also needed in order to create
the magic. When Harry Potter leaves the Ministry of
Magic at the end of a busy day, he walks into a telephone
box, dials 62442 (MAGIC), and disappears. Both sound
and time are important components to the effect.

"There's a certain amount of time Jamie Harrison
knew was involved as Harry walks up to the effect, dials
the phone, the magic happens, and then he disappears,"
Fry explains. "But as soon as he gets to the phone, visually you just see someone in a cloak standing there before
the effect finishes." Fry fills up the ten or so seconds with
a buildup of sounds. "It all comes from speakers nearby,"
he explains, keeping the sound in the location of the
effect. "We've got the voice of the phone bidding 'Fare-
well, Harry Potter,' there's the dialing of the phone and
other sounds from the box, plus Imogen Heap's music
that all build to a crescendo." Followed by a moment of
silence as the audience gasps.

Fry admits that the sounds for the Polyjuice Potion
transformation were also tricky, but proved even more
crucial for lighting designer Neil Austin. The scenes

before and after the transformation required different
lighting, and Austin had to implement quick changes
that wouldn't distract the audience from the illusion.
"And that's where sound helps," says Austin. "Because
as they drink it, *glug, glug, glug*, something happens
immediately, so I could use this *kkkrrrr* sound effect to
go *vvvrrrr* with the lighting. It helps you justify a bigger
change than you would naturally get away with without
any sound."

For the Hogwarts Express, Fry looked into hiring a
steam train to record its sounds. "There are a fair few

that do heritage trips around the country, but when you're doing a sound effects recording you need it to do specific things for you, and maybe three or four times." Fortunately, like the cloaks, Fry found that he had sound effects of various steam trains that were fine to use in the end.

"I remember reading the script for the first time," says Fry, "and quite often when you read a script, you get to a stage direction that might be a paragraph long. The rest is very straightforward, but there's this block of stage directions that's going to be well worth spending all our energy. With *Harry*, you have that on every other page! Now we're on top of a train, now they drink Poly-juice and transform, here we have a malevolent book-case, there's dragons."

Dragons, not surprisingly, weren't already in his database.

• ✳ •

LIGHTING

NEIL AUSTIN LOOKS UPON HIS JOB as a theatrical lighting designer as being similar to five different jobs in filmmaking. "Lighting is a major helping hand in the storytelling of a piece," he explains, "which I can find an equivalency to in filmic terms. The lighting designer is like the director of photography, who chooses what the light should look like. Also, a focus puller, creating a wide shot or a close-up, playing with the depth of space. A colorist, to grade the light to evoke an emotional response from the audience. An editor, finding a way to get from this to that. But I never thought of doing anything other than lighting for the theater." To Austin, lighting the continuous stream of uninterrupted images needed to put on a piece of theater is much more of a challenge.

Austin's resume of West End and Broadway productions includes *Hamlet* with Jude Law, *Macbeth* with Kenneth Branagh, and *Red* with Alfred Molina and Eddie Redmayne, for which he won the 2010 Tony and Drama Desk Awards. The following year he won the Olivier Award for *The White Guard* at the National Theatre.

At the end of a long day working on the Phoenix Theatre's musical production of *Bend It Like Beckham* in 2015, Austin was asked by producer Sonia Friedman to stay behind with her. "We'd had a really tough day on it, starting at nine in the morning," remembers Austin, "and at maybe eleven thirty at night, while doing notes, she just said, 'Oh, can you stay behind and I'll have a word with you?'" He immediately wondered what he'd done wrong and whether or not he was going to be sacked. "She took me out the back and said she really enjoyed what I was doing. Then said, 'What are you doing next year? I'd like you to do Harry Potter.'"

• ✳ •

"LIGHTING GUIDES THE AUDIENCE'S attention, because the audience is always looking at a single wide shot," Austin explains. "Lighting is the thing that helps go, 'Look here, don't look there.' And the 'don't look there' is a very important thing on Harry Potter." Lighting was a key element in achieving every illusion in the show—from Polyjuice transformations to deliveries by owl post—but also contributed significantly to transforming the train station–inspired set as locations shift from scene to scene. "When you're in locations like King's Cross, we have LEDs in the arches so it's big, it's vast, it's tall," says Austin. "But when you're in a smaller environment—the dorm in Hogwarts or McGonagall's office—we just uplight the wainscoting to bring down the height of the set. It's no longer a full-stage picture." The wainscoting lighting was also particularly useful in transforming Hogwarts from one time turn to another. "In the nice version, the wainscoting is lit very, very warm with a lovely candlelight-orange tone. The woodwork Christine chose reacts beautifully to it, so the wood looks glorious and warm and full of depth. For the Dark-world version of Hogwarts, it's lit in a very steely, silvery blue and goes monochromatic, so it almost seems as if you're looking at a black-and-white image," Austin explains.

The choice of color palette within the lighting can set not just place, but time. "That's time in terms of time of day, but also time as in are we in the now or are we in the then," says Austin. For their final time turn, Albus and Scorpius need to go to Godric's Hollow in 1981, the place where Harry was born and his parents were killed. The small town is defined by a row of five doors, each with a distinct color. Godric's Hollow is also seen in the present day, before Harry, Ginny, Hermione, Ron, and Draco time-turn back in an effort save the boys. "We needed to show a difference in the look of those five doors," says Austin. His decision was to enhance the color on each of the doors in the present day. "I wanted to really ping them. A red light would go on

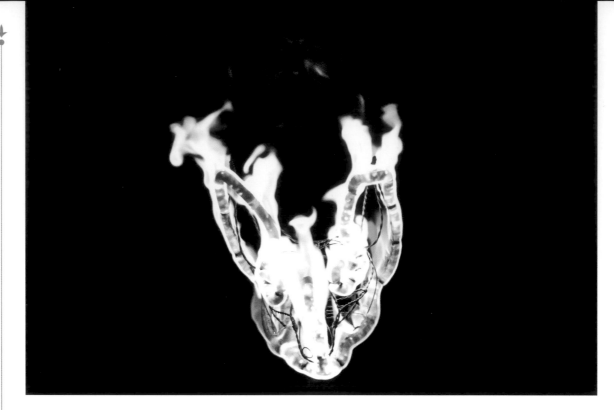

a red door, a blue light on blue, and so on," Austin explains. "It made them vivid." Within the time turn, the doors' colors are gently muted. "They still have color, but it feels old-fashioned, like an old postcard that's faded."

Conversely, for Albus and Scorpius's visits to the Triwizard Tournament earlier in the show, the past is given a hyperrealistic look. "You need to give the audience the visual clues," Austin explains. "So, each time we time-turn there, the audience picks up that we're back in that super hypercolored world, so okay, we're back in the past."

Another tool in Austin's lighting kit that communicates time, place, and mood is haze. Harry Potter's dreams have not only a distinctive color palette but a unique haze palette. "That smoke and the way it's lit helps the audience recognize that when they get to one of those scenes, it isn't the present day, this isn't time-turning to the past; this is one of Harry's dreams."

· ✳ ·

"I'LL TELL YOU, I GOT A LOT OF EXERcise," Austin says with a laugh. "Normally when you light a show, you sit maybe halfway back in the auditorium, very much anchored to your headset and your computer and your programmer, looking at the image onstage." For *Harry Potter and the Cursed Child*, Austin was constantly taking off the headset and running up the stairs to the balconies to check every possible sightline for the show's many complex illusions. "Doesn't matter what seat you're in, doesn't matter how much you've paid for your ticket, doesn't matter whether you're under the dress

circle, whether you're right at the very front or at the back," he states. "What we've got to make sure is that everybody in the auditorium gets that sense of 'Wow, I'm in the middle of it.' And 'How on earth has that been hidden from me for the last three acts?'"

· ✳ ·

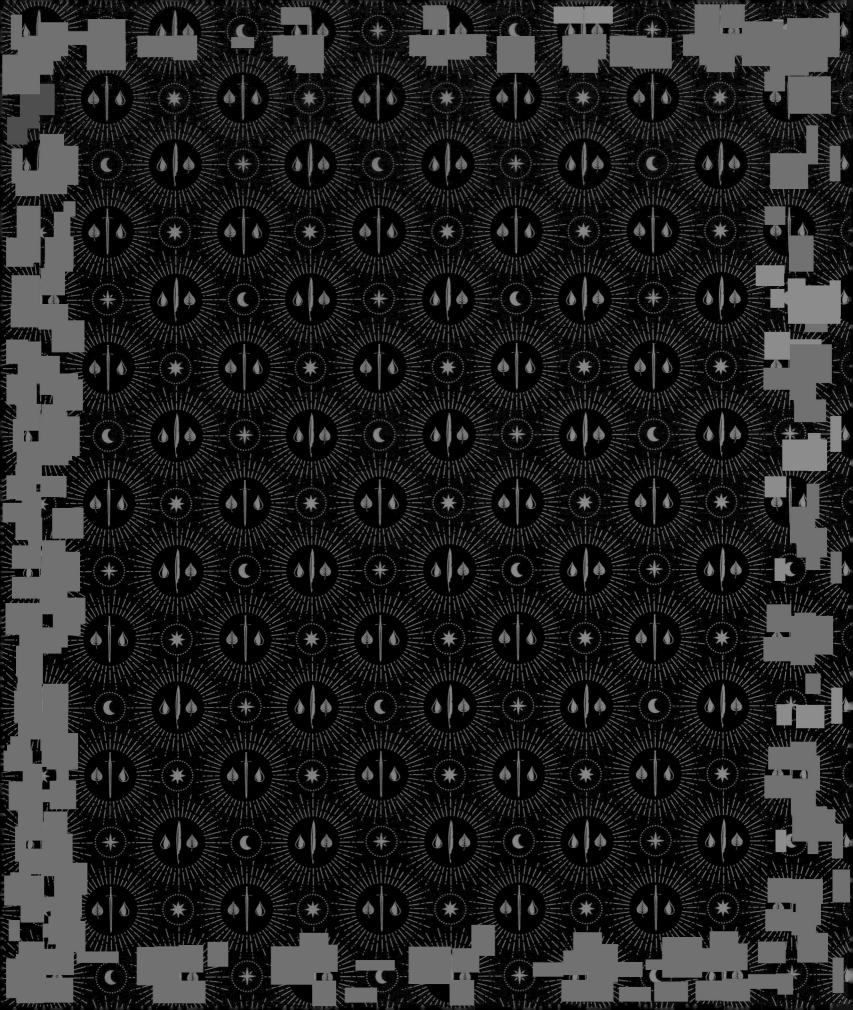

CHAPTER

5

MOVING INTO THE

PALACE

URING THE SUMMER OF 2015, Sonia Friedman, Colin Callender, and John Tiffany searched for a West End theater that would become Harry's new home. It took less than a handful of assessments before the Palace Theatre, set behind a small plaza at the intersection of Shaftesbury Avenue and Charing Cross Road, was chosen. Everyone on the team knew of the theater from *Les Misérables*, among many other productions performed there. And, "the Palace kind of looks like Hogwarts," says Tiffany. "It's a beautiful, deep-rooted standalone building, of which there are only about three in London. That felt right, and the outside of it felt right, so it was really obvious to me that we should try and get here." Friedman reached out to theater owner Nica Burns of Nimax. "She agreed that the Palace would be the perfect home for Harry Potter in the West End and made it available for us," says Friedman.

"Because the Palace is a listed building, there were lots of rules and regulations we had to adhere to," says Des Kennedy. "It was very delicate how we turned the Palace into Hogwarts." One way was what Brett J. Banakis calls "moments of discovery." Although there was already beautiful ornamentation in the theater—gilded cherubs on walls and balconies, arched columns, and a three-story chandelier lighting system—the creative team wanted to add their own touches.

So Christine Jones and Banakis developed different shaped dragon sconces to place throughout the theater. "We had a sconce for each of the different houses," says Jones. Additionally, Tiffany wanted the entrance to the Palace to evoke a train station, so the stars and moons seen on the stage's proscenium were echoed on the exterior canopy. "John, Sonia, and Colin chose the Palace because it already resembled Hogwarts," says Kennedy. "So, it was just about bringing out its Hogwarts energy, which was already there, rather than having to change anything."

"You shouldn't ignore the threshold that the audience walks through, or what is beyond it before they find their seat," says Tiffany. "It says to them, 'Things might happen here.' It puts them in a different sense of alertness, as opposed to the safeness of going to see a West End or Broadway musical. There they think, 'Nothing's going to happen apart from what will be seen onstage, which is going to be brilliant.' But if you start to change the color of the lights or make the ushers look slightly different than typically seen, it's almost like the audience's skin becomes slightly rawer and their nerves become slightly sharper. The second you walk into the theater, you should think, 'Okay, anything can happen here.'"

• ✳ •

{ right }

From left, international scenic supervisor Brett J. Banakis, set designer Christine Jones, and international technical director Gary Beestone at the Palace Theatre

{ left }

Cast, crew, and
creative and
production teams
in technical
rehearsals at the
Palace Theatre

{ next page }

The Palace Theatre
in the West End,
London

{ *above* }

Director John Tiffany with the cast during technical rehearsals at the Palace Theatre

ONCE DESIGN CHANGES WERE IMPLE-mented at the Palace Theatre, dry tech rehearsals for the show could begin. Dry tech has the technical team running through the show cue by cue, without the actors. "It's specifically looking at all the larger technical moments that involve automation or flying, anything that involves specialists. Otherwise, if you waited for the actors to come in, there'd be a lot of hanging about," says Friedman. The moment dry tech is completed, the company leaves the rehearsal room, where they've been doing run-throughs without flying or trap work, and joins the technical team that has been there already for several weeks. "This is the commencement of technical rehearsals—tech," she explains. "Tech goes through the show, scene by scene, hour by hour. And once we start tech, we know that in five weeks' time at seven p.m., we have one thousand three hundred and sixty people walking through the door to see the first preview."

Friedman finds this part of the process very exciting. "It's the first time you see Hagrid walk onstage—and, whoa! It's the first time I saw the transition from St. Oswald's into the Ministry, with Imogen Heap's music, Gareth Fry's sound, and Steven Hoggett's movement with Katrina Lindsay's cloaks—I didn't see that in rehearsal, and it was just the most beautiful transition."

Producer Colin Callender felt that by the time everyone had moved into the theater, there was what he would characterize as an esprit de corps. "There was a sense we were going through a communal experience that was very powerful. By the time we actually finished the rehearsals and went into that theater, everyone was on a mission and at every level wanted to do their finest work."

• ✳ •

AFTER YEARS OF PLANNING, DEVELOP-ment, workshops, and rehearsals, in June 2016 it was time at last to perform the show for an audience. "We had had this special secret," says Fiona Stewart, associate producer at Sonia Friedman Productions, "and it was really exciting knowing that only the people in the rehearsal room or inside the theater during tech knew it at the time. But on the day we had our first audience, it was even more exciting because we were opening the doors and sharing it with a big family that was joining us."

On June 6, 2016, the production held a dress rehearsal before an invited audience of friends and family. It was also the first time J.K. Rowling had seen the play fully staged in front of an audience. "What we had in that room was a thousand people who were completely transfixed by what was happening in front of them, something that has meant something huge and emotional to all of them, me very much included, and we were all united in this experience. It was remarkable," Rowling recalls.

"Honestly, the first time this play was on, the first preview, it was like a rock concert," says playwright Jack Thorne. "It was unreal. When Hermione said, 'I'm the Minister for Magic,' the whole audience went, '*Aaaahhhhhh!*'"

"We knew people were going to be interested," says Noma Dumezweni (Hermione Granger), "but before we even started the thing, the energy was palpable in the auditorium. When Chris Jarman, the Sorting Hat, gave the opening announcement, saying, 'Please put your cell phones away, and I mean now,' it was like, whoa!" Not surprisingly, the audience was reacting to every single word. "We all looked at each other and thought, *Oh my god, here we go!*"

Paul Thornley (Ron Weasley) calls the first preview "insane. There was press from all around the world and the most supercharged Harry Potter fans you've ever seen. We'd been in this little rehearsal bubble, out in the middle of east London in this aircraft hangar for twelve weeks, thinking we were doing a little play. We'd sort of forgotten that we were doing Harry Potter. And then suddenly the world's press is there and people dressed as wizards. The noise was unlike anything I've ever experienced."

"The whole buildup was huge, because it was this much awaited product," says Poppy Miller (Ginny Potter), "and at the same time, people were waiting to like it or not like it—that was a very real possibility. We were pretty sure they would like it, but we didn't know how it would be received by the fans and the critics. And it was all very exciting."

Alex Price (Draco Malfoy) has a slightly different memory of the first preview. "The thing that I remember most is, *Don't screw it up*," he says with a laugh. "I remember the noise just before curtain went up, and as Jamie came on as Harry, as everybody went onto that stage. But from then on, I was like, *Head down, don't miss a beat. Don't fall over, don't hit the furniture*."

"The previews," sums up Jamie Parker (Harry Potter), "were unforgettable."

• ✳ •

"PREVIEWS ARE THE FINAL PIECE OF this process," says Friedman. "Ultimately, you learn everything from your audience and how they're responding. Timings and energy and rhythms of pieces. You can sense in an audience when they're looking at their watch. You can feel the moment when you've lost their attention. But you have to go through previews to know that. That's when a lot of work happens."

Thorne paid special attention to how the audiences were reacting and continued to hone the script during the preview period. "With new writing, typically, the script doesn't get 'frozen' until you have press performances," says Diane Benjamin of SFP. "Because a script is meant to be performed, so you're not going to get a proper feel of it until you get thirteen hundred people watching it."

In addition to dialogue changes, adjustments were made to lighting, sound, and other technical elements, including the illusions.

"People would come up to our desk in tech and say, 'Oh, I think you can tell how that trick is done,'" illusion designer Jamie Harrison remembers. "Or, 'It didn't look very magical to me this time. What's happened?' While at the same time, Chris and I were thinking the illusion

A BADGE OF HONOR

• ✳ •

#KeepTheSecrets

Though the press would not be allowed to see the show on the first night of previews, the producers received advance notice that news teams and camera crews would be outside the theater. "We thought, What's going to happen?" producer Colin Callender recalls. "Audience members at the end of Part One, which was shown on Wednesday night, are going to leave the theater and there will be TV crews outside, who'd be asking, 'What's it like? What's the show like?'" That's when the idea of the Keep the Secrets badges came up. "We already had the tagline 'Keep the Secrets.' So, as the audience left the first preview, they were handed a Keep the Secrets badge. When the TV crews would ask, 'What's the story?' they could point to the badge. It was hysterical and absolutely wonderful. That badge really became a badge of honor."

had looked better than it ever had. That was a difficult moment and took a lot of resilience to get through." Harrison explains that there's a certain skill in seeing the magic in an effect when you've seen it a hundred times. "It often happens in the journey of bringing illusions to stage that when people see an effect the first few times, they love it, and then they fall out of love with it because they've seen it so often." He tried to explain to the doubters that this was part of the process, "but it was a lot of pressure for everybody. This wasn't a show that was going to go under the radar." When the first audiences came in, and "gasped and cheered and clapped," says Harrison, "it was a really emotional release for me to see them responding the way we'd hoped."

• ✳ •

"I DON'T THINK THERE WERE ANY BIG surprises by the time we began previews at the Palace," says producer Colin Callender. "Except for the owl."

While Harry, Ginny, Ron, and Hermione have dinner in the kitchen of the Potter house to discuss the problems of the day, an owl swoops in to deliver a message from Professor McGonagall. "For the first preview, we had a real owl," Callender explains. There were, in fact, two scenes where owls were to deliver messages: the kitchen scene in Act One, and later on when Albus sends a message to Delphi in Act Two. Trainers came in during tech to teach the birds—a barn owl and a barred owl—their behaviors. The barn owl was McGonagall's and would fly into the kitchen and land on a chair, Harry would take the note, and the owl would fly into the wings. Albus's owl would fly in from the wings, land on his leather-gloved arm, then fly off into the auditorium.

At the dress rehearsal, the owls mostly behaved as they should have. For the first preview, however, the owl flew to its Act Two mark instead of its Act One mark and became confused. So it landed near the audience on the circle front. The owl's handlers were able to move it away from the audience, but not out of the auditorium. Eventually, the owl landed at the top of an arch onstage. "What was brilliant was it landed so specifically there that it looked almost intentional," says Pam Skinner. But, of course, the audience became more interested in the owl than what was happening onstage. During intermission, the owl was safely recovered—and retired—as Tiffany made an easy decision for going forward: "No live owls in this show anymore, thank you."

• ✳ •

{ *right* }

Sam Clemmett
(Albus Potter)
backstage at the
Palace Theatre

{ *left* }

Anthony Boyle
(Scorpius Malfoy)
and Alex Price
(Draco Malfoy)
backstage at the
Palace Theatre

OPENING DAY

· ✳ ·

THE OPENING OF *HARRY POTTER AND the Cursed Child* should probably be called opening day and night, as both parts of the show were staged in a single day on July 30, 2016.

For the gala performance, a red carpet was laid in front of the Palace Theatre and down Romilly Street on one side. Roads were closed to traffic, fans filled the plaza in front of the theater, and press interviews were given in front of the theater before Part One. "We had tons of TV crews, photographers, entertainment reporters, and news reporters," says Janine Shalom, press rep for the London production of *Cursed Child*. Reports appeared on the evening news, the late evening news, and the next morning's news. "And people were keeping the secrets," she continues. "Nothing was being given away, not even from the critics."

After the final bow, where J.K. Rowling joined a curtain call with the cast, everyone was taken on private red London buses for a gala party in the Booking Office, the bar at the St. Pancras Hotel, and the room that had inspired the design of the set. A DJ booth was made from suitcases, and a few pieces of set dressing were used as seats. The lighting gave a nod to the House colors.

"I remember being at the Booking Office with Brett Banakis and he asked me if I recognized anything on the walls," says Meg Massey, *Cursed Child*'s head of marketing. "It was the set! Some of it's just exactly the same and it was amazing. I hadn't realized how closely they'd taken it from the real thing."

At midnight, critics' reviews started pouring in, and a special rehearsal edition of the playscript went on sale across the world. Bookstores stayed open late for the occasion, recalling the midnight book parties from the release of the original Harry Potter novels. "I remember after the party a lot of us ran to the nearest bookshop in King's Cross to buy the book," says Fiona Stewart. For everyone, the secret was finally out. "I could talk about it now," says Stewart. "The whole night was incredible."

• ✳ •

{ above }

Sonia Friedman, Jack Thorne, J.K. Rowling, John Tiffany, and Colin Callender on the red carpet on opening night

{ below }

The creative team and cast during the opening night performance and curtain call

AND THE AWARD
GOES TO...

• ✳ •

THE EXTRAORDINARY WORK DONE BY the cast and crew was rewarded by sellout crowds, glowing reviews, and, ultimately, a record-breaking number of awards. In addition to nominations and wins at the WhatsOnStage Awards, the Critics' Circle Theatre Awards, and the Evening Standard Theatre Awards, the show won nine Olivier Awards—the most ever for a play—including Best Director (John Tiffany), Best Set Design (Christine Jones), Best Lighting Design (Neil Austin), Best Sound Design (Gareth Fry), Best Costume Design (Katrina Lindsay), Best Actor (Jamie Parker), Best Actor in a Supporting Role (Anthony Boyle), Best Actress in a Supporting Role (Noma Dumezweni), and Best New Play.

• ✳ •

{ *far right* }

Jamie Parker (Harry Potter) and Noma Dumezweni (Hermione Granger) at the 2017 Olivier Awards

{ *near right* }

Clockwise; set designer Christine Jones, director John Tiffany, and playwright Jack Thorne with their Olivier Awards

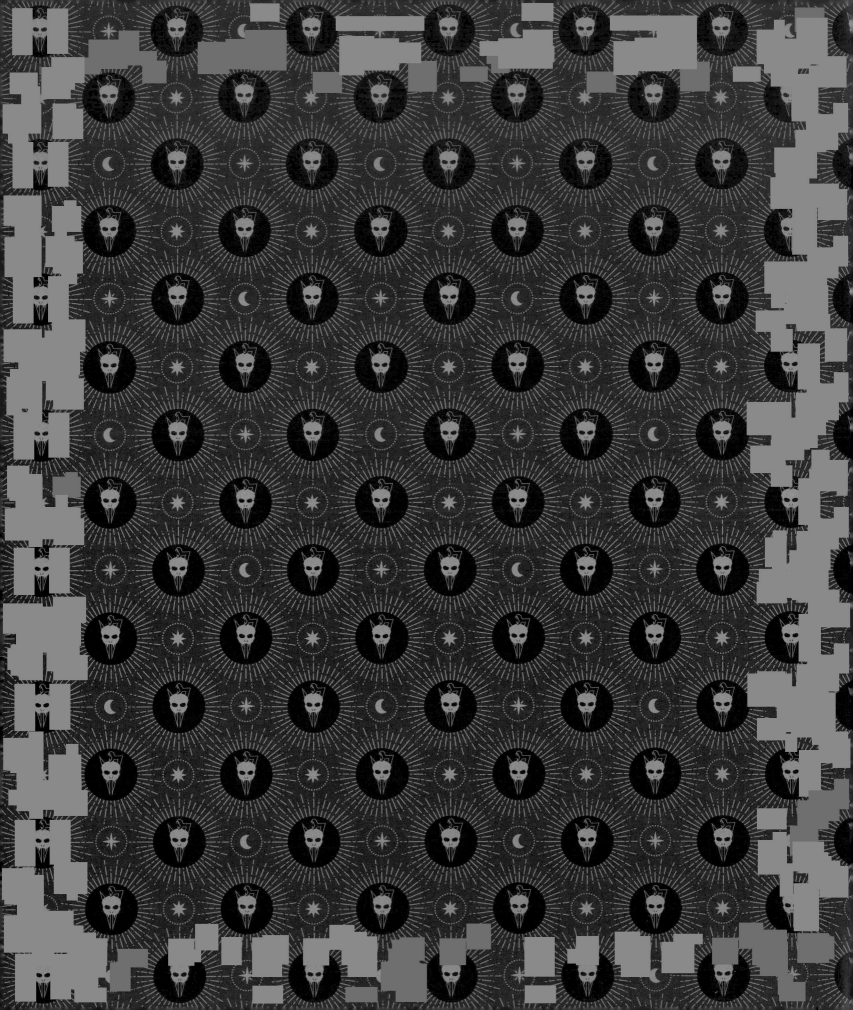

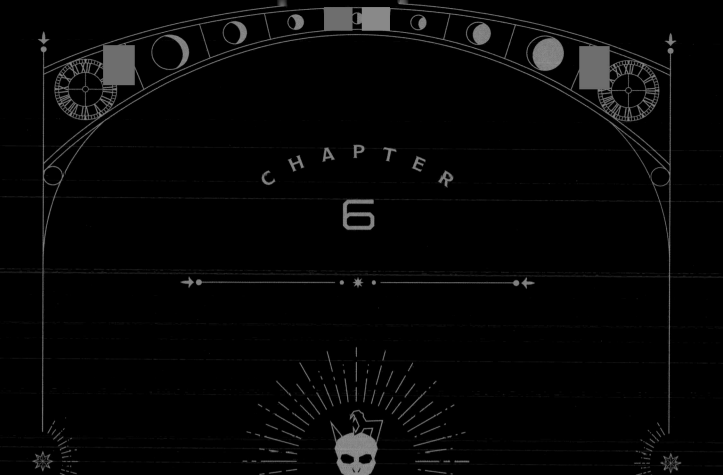

CHAPTER

6

BROADWAY

BOUND

AFTER THE OPENING OF *HARRY POTTER and the Cursed Child* in the West End, talk soon turned to taking the production to Broadway. "Sonia and I are both independently extremely superstitious," says Colin Callender. "It just happens we're both the same way in this regard—we were very loath to get ahead of ourselves in terms of discussing New York before the play opened." But about five months after the West End opening, it was announced that *Cursed Child* would be going to Broadway in 2018, following a major renovation of the Lyric Theatre.

Christine Jones remembers a conversation she had with John Tiffany when they were first assessing the space. "John and I talked about the soul of the theater," she says. "When one of the previous shows was in here, they gutted the floor. When the production was halted because it needed to raise more money, the theater sat there with this gaping wound for months. We felt that maybe they had actually hurt the theater. So part of what we wanted to do was heal it and love it. But it wasn't a completely blank slate. We wanted to build a new theater within the old theater, not completely eradicate what had been there before."

The 1996 Lyric was described by the *New York Times* as a "charmless barn of a theater," and Broadway producers were known to say that the voluminous auditorium swallowed up shows. Therefore, one of the most crucial objectives for the producers and the set design team was to establish a more intimate space. To that end, four hundred seats were removed and a new back wall to the auditorium was constructed, eliminating rows on the orchestra level that were too far from the stage. In the dress circle, four rows were added to bring the first balcony level that much closer to the action.

The designers also drew on the vocabulary of the set design as they looked for more ways to adjust the auditorium. "We didn't want to re-create the stage," says Jones, "and we didn't want the theater to look like an exact

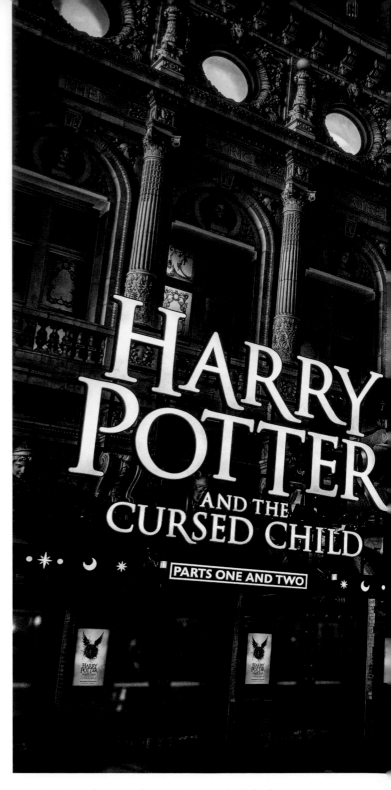

extension in a theme park-y way. But we had the language of the arches and it was a pretty quick realization that if we did extend the arches into the house, it would bring the ceiling down, which addressed the overall goal of making the whole space feel more intimate."

The ceiling of the auditorium now gives one the feeling of being in the Great Hall in Hogwarts, with undulating beams and arches. The design also solved an issue that has plagued theater productions for years. "In older

{ *left* }

The façade of the Lyric Theatre, home of *Harry Potter and the Cursed Child* on Broadway

{ *next page* }

Auditorium of the Lyric Theatre, custom redesigned for *Cursed Child*

theaters, the way they lit productions was very different," explains Jones. "Usually, you have trusses that are exposed. You can try to mask them, but only to a certain extent." In addition to lighting, trusses can hold video, audio, or other stage equipment. "To have the opportunity to go in ahead of time, figure out where the lighting needed to be, and be able to build that all within the architecture meant that we were able to create an environment where much less of that equipment is visible."

For *Harry Potter and the Cursed Child*, not only are lights concealed within the barrel-vault ceiling, but speakers and equipment for effects and illusions as well. "What we were able to do in this theater we'll probably never be able to do again," says Gary Beestone. "Being able to custom design the theater rather than having to deal with what you've got was a major win."

• ❋ •

{ *right* }

Details of the redesigned auditorium and lobby at the Lyric Theatre:

"We decided to design the sconces in the auditorium as phoenixes because of the idea that the Lyric is a theater that has fallen and risen out of the flames," explains set designer Christine Jones.

{ *left* }

The lobby of the renovated Lyric Theatre featuring a Patronus mural by artist Peter Strain

{ *below* }

The ceiling of the lobby at the Lyric Theatre, featuring the moon-and-star motif from Christine Jones's set design, and owls in flight

THE THEATER RENOVATION DIDN'T STOP at the auditorium, however. "The audience's experience begins the moment they step into the lobby," says Friedman. "It was important to bring the atmosphere of the Harry Potter world into those front-of-house spaces."

"We wanted the audience to walk in and feel as if they were in a mysterious place," says Jones. Custom wallpaper—originally designed for the Palace Theatre by Jones and Banakis—features the Hogwarts *H*, as well as symbols for each of the houses: a feather for Ravenclaw, a sword for Gryffindor, a leaf for Hufflepuff, and a drop for Slytherin, "which I interpreted as either venom or blood, depending on how you want to look at it," says Jones. In addition to wallpaper and other details in the theater, the Hogwarts *H* containing the house symbols was used for the lobby and upper floors' carpet.

"I really believe that part of the success of the experience in New York is the theater," says Callender. "Certainly, there were lots of tightropes that we walked at every step of the way. But I think the right balance was struck in that the moment you walk through the door of the theater, it's of the world but not a theme park. When you step over the threshold of the theater, you will be entering the world of Harry Potter."

• ✳ •

A SECOND BEGINNING

• ✳ •

HARRY POTTER AND THE CURSED CHILD began previews on March 16, then opened on April 22, 2018. "In London, nobody knew what to expect, so the sense of discovery of the show in London was glorious," says Callender. "The challenge we had in coming to New York was that it had already got these great reviews in London, it was already a big hit, it had already won nine Oliviers. So our challenge was living up to those expectations."

Seven members of the original West End Company had committed to the first year on Broadway: Jamie Parker (Harry), Poppy Miller (Ginny), Paul Thornley (Ron), Noma Dumezweni (Hermione), Alex Price (Draco), Sam Clemmett (Albus), and Anthony Boyle (Scorpius). They were joined onstage by a diverse company of American actors for the North American premiere of the play.

"It was always a no-brainer," says Clemmett. "It was daunting to begin with, knowing we'd do it for another year, but I'm so pleased we did." Clemmett and other actors felt that even after all the time they had spent in the roles, there was still unfinished business, which became obvious to the young actor when they began rehearsals in New York. "We all had new ideas, fresh ideas when we read the script again." Jack Thorne was back in the rehearsal room again, as was John Tiffany. "John was brilliant at giving us a clean slate for the first rehearsal we did in New York," Clemmett remembers. "For two and a half hours, we just talked it through, down to minute details that we never got to do in London, because we just ran out of time there. We all wanted it to keep developing—that's just what art is."

Steven Hoggett looked at opportunities for changes in the movement due not only to the Lyric being a different size, but also because with a new company, new viewpoints are heard during rehearsals. "Something is dead certain for you, and then you get asked that one question," he explains. "So, you're like, yeah, actually, let's just have a think about that. We've always benefited from new questions being asked."

• ✳ •

NEW YORK AUDIENCES ARE KNOWN FOR being a bit more boisterous than British ones. "They are intense," says Dumezweni. "And in the best way."

"The weirdest thing was that they clap upon people's entrances here, which doesn't happen in the UK as much," adds Thornley. "And some comment more. But if people are involved in something, I don't have a problem with that. I quite like it."

New York audiences embraced the production, as did the critics. When the Broadway theater awards season came around, *Harry Potter and the Cursed Child* won five Drama Desk Awards, six Outer Critics Circle Awards, and six Tony Awards, for Best Play, Best Direction of a Play, Best Scenic Design, Best Costume Design, Best Lighting Design, and Best Sound Design.

• ✳ •

{ below }

Producers Colin Callender and Sonia Friedman, playwright Jack Thorne, and cast onstage at the 2018 Tony Awards

THE JOURNEY

CONTINUES

LIKE ANY THEATRICAL PRODUCTION, the hope is that *Harry Potter and the Cursed Child* will reach the widest possible audience, expanding across the globe and bringing Harry's eighth story to superfans, new fans, and new audiences, whether in London, New York, Melbourne, San Francisco, Hamburg, Toronto, or beyond.

"This show is a living, breathing organism; every production has its own identity," says international associate director Des Kennedy. Adjustments are made to the set, the costumes, even the script. New casts are chosen for each new production, with cast changes occurring each year. "Every time you re-rehearse it, the actors will find new things," says Sonia Friedman. "Each cast is completely different and equally brilliant. And I love seeing it through these actors, because it is genuinely very different each time." Kennedy adds, "I think I would go mad if my job was to tell an actor to say it like this, because five years ago Jamie Parker stood there and said it like that. Actors have to interpret this in their own way, and we have to make their own version of the show."

And then there's the unique energy the audience brings to each performance. "Not everybody comes with full knowledge of Harry Potter, but a large percentage of our audience members come with a deep love of this world, and so the energy in the room is unlike anything that I've experienced in other productions," says set designer Christine Jones. "It truly is unique. The quality and personality of the audience, night to night, really does change the chemistry and the alchemy of what happens for every show."

"Sometimes we can have really quiet houses and the actors think that they're doing a terrible show," says Friedman. "The audience isn't laughing, or they're not responding, or they're not applauding the illusions. But then the roar at the end can sometimes be greater than the audiences that give a lot of response. There are audiences that get into a rhythm of just listening, and there are audiences that get into the rhythm of responding. There really is no knowing which one it's going to end up being before it starts. And, of course, it affects everything."

For the London production, "we knew that at least sixty percent of the audience has never booked a theater ticket before," says Meg Massey of Sonia Friedman Productions. "And a huge percentage of those brand-new theatergoers have gone on to book tickets for more shows." Kennedy comments that many decisions for the show were made with that first-time theatergoer in mind. "We hoped to do with theater what Jo did with books—bring reading to a whole new generation. We wanted to bring theater to a whole new generation."

As part of the effort to make the show accessible to new theatergoers, the producers initiated the Friday Forty, a weekly lottery for forty fans to purchase inexpensive tickets (in prime seat locations) to that weekend's shows. How did they come up with the name? "We've never really said this, but the reason we chose forty tickets," Massey explains, "was in honor of the 'original forty,' the first forty student names J.K. Rowling came up with and listed when writing the first book."

The fact that so many of the audience members are first-time theatergoers is thrilling to the producers and creative team. "If they're fans, they're bringing their own history and emotional connection to Harry into the theater," says producer Colin Callender. "They're meeting characters again that they loved and haven't seen for a while, who have moved on, as they themselves have moved on. So, the play is, in many ways, about growing up, because the audience that comes to see *Cursed Child* has grown up with Harry, as the characters onstage have

grown up. Therefore, this audience has a very special relationship with what's onstage.

"Being a member of the audience and being aware of the audience around you is part of the whole experience of seeing *Cursed Child*, more so than any play I've ever been an audience member of," Callender continues. "Half the fun of watching the play is actually watching the audience and how they react to certain moments." Friedman agrees wholeheartedly: "The audiences with Harry, they bring energy, they have the reactions, they have the responses, they have waves of laughter, but they also have waves of recognition, of a sense of home. Harry's back."

Friedman reflects that one of the most rewarding aspects of working in live theater is the audience. "And with it, the formation of a community," she explains. "Theater needs to be a place where people come together and go on a shared experience together. That experience can be emotional, it can be cathartic, it can be political, it can be a rallying cry, it can be angry. But the best theater is if you come in as one person and you leave as a slightly different one." Friedman continues, "You look at the world in a slightly different way, but you turn to the person next to you and you grin at them and you've made a new friend, and you've made a new connection. The best theater is when you arrive as individuals and you leave as one."

{ *above* }

The Princess Theatre in Melbourne, Australia

{ *below* }

Audience for *Harry Potter and the Cursed Child* at the Princess Theatre

{ *left* }

New cast members from the London, New York, and Melbourne productions of *Harry Potter and the Cursed Child*

ACKNOWLEDGMENTS

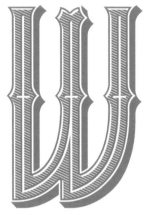

E WISH WE HAD ANOTHER thousand pages to fill with photographs and memories of all the incredible people who have made this production happen. We tried to list them all, but there are too many to count! At last tally, it was well over a thousand people, in cities all across the world. Each and every one of them, whether they were there with us at the start of it all and still are, or whether they were with us for a short time, each and every one is a part of our *Cursed Child* family and always will be.

All of our actors past, present, and future, the creative teams, production management company and stage management, costume, "WHAM," lighting, illusions, automa-

tion, sound and music, design assistants, props, set builders, contractors, theater owners and theater staff both backstage and front of house, all of the teams at SFP, Playground, and The Blair Partnership, our general management teams, marketing agencies, press agents, photographers and videographers, our suppliers, rehearsal spaces, and even, or perhaps especially, our cake bakers!

And of course to all Harry Potter fans, for whom we tell this story, and our amazing, amazing audiences who go on this incredible adventure with us, day after day. We couldn't do this without you, and we're eternally grateful to each and every one of you for keeping Harry Potter's world alive in your hearts.

—Sonia & Colin

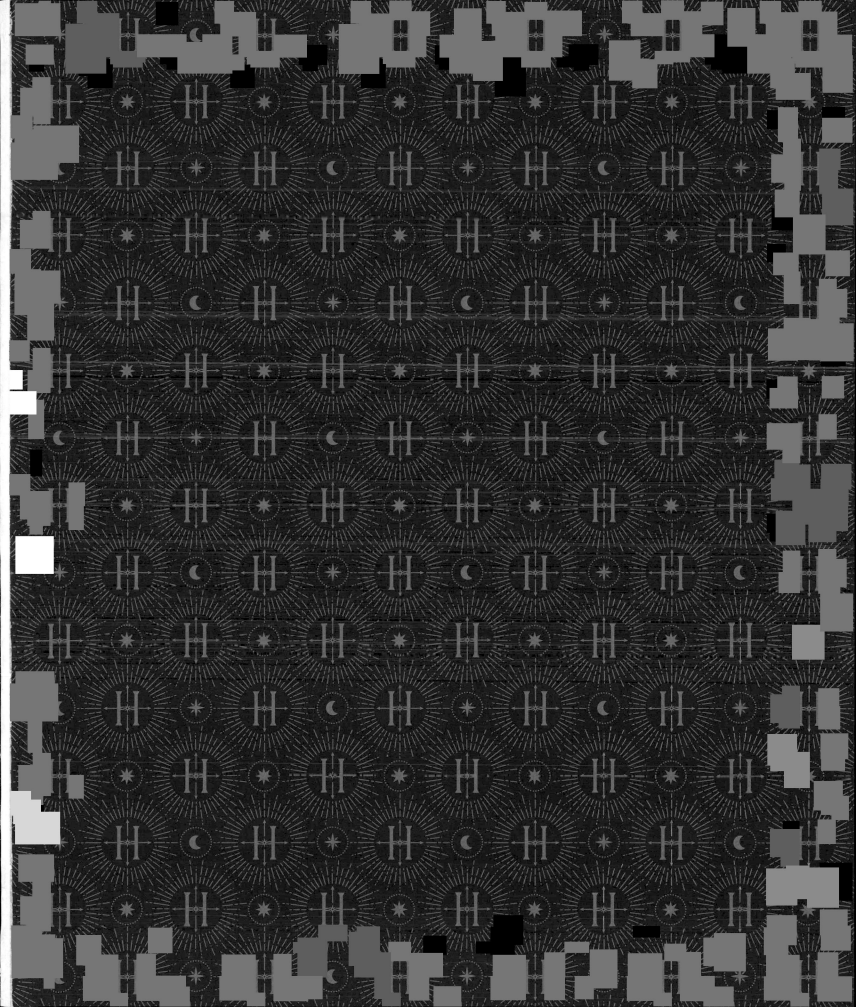